DIAMOND T TRUCKS
1911-1966 PHOTO ARCHIVE

Robert Gabrick

Iconografix

Iconografix
PO Box 446
Hudson, Wisconsin 54016 USA

Library of Congress Control Number: 2007932532

ISBN-10: 1-58388-204-9
ISBN-13: 978-1-58388-204-7

07 08 09 10 11 12 6 5 4 3 2 1

Printed in China

Cover and book design by Dan Perry

Cover photo- "Whenever men talk trucks, sooner or later the topic turns to Diamond T's new gas jobs. Why? Because these Diamond T's earn more…get better gas mileage, have snappier performance and require less maintenance. Each is custom built to fit the job, and each has Diamond T quality from bumper to rear crossmember." This advertising copy from *Commercial Car Journal*, January 1961 introduced the new two-axle 4000 Series and the three-axle 4300 Series models. Diamond T, a division of the White Motor Company along with Reo, used a Reo cab for these models. Sales literature noted the "all steel die-formed and welded 'R' cab is designed for maximum driver comfort and convenience." The full 63 3/16-inch wide cab was "weather-proof, rattle-free and is insulated against heat, cold, and noise." The cab was equipped with a "Luxurious, full width seat…covered in heavy calf-grain vinyl." Buyers of the 23,500 to 50,000 pound GVW model shown above had the choice of the standard Reo-built Super Service 145 HP 331-ci 6-cylinder DT6-145, and the optional 331-ci 6-cylinder 170 HP DT6-170 or the DT6-185 362-ci 6-cylinder 185 HP engines. Diamond T emphasized their replaceable wet-sleeve cylinder liners. "Wet sleeves are true cylinders, machined inside and out, free from warping and distortion. At overhaul time—you don't. You rebuild to original factory dimensions and tolerances at far less cost than a rebore job." *Michigan State University Archives and Historical Collections*

Dedication

To the memory of my mother, Helen, 1912-2007

People often ask why and how I became interested in trucks. I believe that part of this passion is innate; its origins as mysterious as any other tendency nurtured since childhood. Part of the credit must go to my mother who encouraged her sons to pursue their passions, regardless of convention. She and my father also had the wisdom to have the family live near two truck routes starting when I was only six months old. The many enjoyable hours I spent watching, listening, and even smelling those wonderful trucks rumbling down Franklin Avenue and East 26th Street in Minneapolis cannot fully resolve the age-old nature vs. nurture debate.

Acknowledgements

A highlight of my research activities was the opportunity to meet with Eric Wentworth, the grandson of C.A. "Art" Tilt, the founder of the Diamond T Motor Car Company. Eric's recollections of his grandfather and his own adventures, while sometimes beyond the scope of this book, were delightful. Eric's collection of Diamond T information, photographs, and family mementoes were important to my research.

Lon Arbegust provided access to his extensive collection of Diamond T materials and photographs. A significant portion of the photographs in this book are from his collection.

Leroy Gurganus provided photographs and materials from his personal collection.

The staff at the Detroit Public Library, and in particular Barbara Thompson, arranged for the use of the Diamond T photographs in the superb National Automotive History Collection. These photographs are prominent in this book.

Frederick L. Honhart, the Director of the University Archives and Historical Collections, and the Archives staff of the Michigan State University Archives, East Lansing, Michigan, insured the availability of essential photographs.

At the marvelous Nethercutt Automotive Research Library, Sylmar, California, Curator and Archivist Skip Marketti, Staff Archivist Lori Thornhill, as well as Kimberly Zarceno once again provided assistance, support, and of course access to the library's collection of material related to Diamond T.

My friend and colleague, Barbara Markham was my indispensable research partner at the Library of Congress, Washington, DC.

The primary source materials I used were essential to providing accurate information about Diamond T. While relying on the expertise and assistance of many, I alone am responsible for the factual accuracy and interpretations of this book.

It would be unfortunate if the reader would not realize the significant amount of history this "Photo Archive" book contains. Do not be deceived by the impression that this book is merely a collection of photographs. The captions, as I have noted in previous books, are "vehicles to tell the larger story." Each of these "vehicles" is the result of extensive research that tells the story of the vehicle in the photograph, but more importantly, also provides significant historical information.

Diamond T sales literature, quoted extensively, provides a wonderful window onto the flavor of the times, offering a glimpse into the minds of those who sought to convince potential customers that a Diamond T was *the* truck to purchase, whether it was "The Nation's Freight Car," "The Handsomest Truck in America," or "The Truck of Lowest Cost."

The history of Diamond T trucks is also about people. We can and must acknowledge prominent individuals such as C.A. Tilt, the founder of the Diamond T Motor Car Company, the public face of Diamond T. We cannot as easily do the same for the numerous men and women who played other parts in the Diamond T story. They were workers on assembly lines, technicians behind a desk doing design or engineering work, dealers shaking hands with clients taking delivery of a new Diamond T, or a driver at the wheel of a truck at work. It is important to remember that each played a significant role in the story of Diamond T.

This book contains some Diamond Reo photographs. Their primary purpose is to illustrate the initial continuity the White Motor Corporation maintained following the introduction of the merged brands. The Diamond Reo story is beyond the scope of this book.

Introduction

1905-1919

The June 28, 1947 issue of the *Diamond T Compass* was the "C.A. Tilt Birthday Issue." A key article was "Forty-two Years of Diamond T Progress." The hero of this "Romance of American Business" was the company's founder. The article offered this assessment: "It has been aptly said by some observer that nearly every great business is really 'the lengthened shadow of one man.' And if it had not been said before, the phrase might have been coined to describe Diamond T and its founder and lifetime leader, C.A. Tilt."

Nine years later, in the 1956 *Annual Report*, a memorial tribute to C.A. Tilt adopted by the Diamond T Board of Directors reprised the theme of the "lengthened shadow."

"On September 19, 1956 our Almighty Father called to his eternal reward Charles Arthur Tilt, the founder and chief executive officer of the Diamond T Motor Car Company from its inception.

Thus passed from the stage of the great automotive industry one of its true pioneers, who had carved for himself and his company a reputation of accomplishment second to none.

Due to Mr. Tilt's constant efforts, the Diamond T name is known and respected throughout the length and breadth of our land, and in most of the important truck markets all over the world. From a modest beginning he built Diamond T into a sound and enduring organization—and it is today the only remaining company of its type from more than a thousand which entered and past out of the motor truck industry.

But more important in the memories of his host of friends will live Charles Arthur Tilt—the man. His adherence to the highest ideals of business ethics, his great understanding of human problems, his ability to command the respect and loyalty of all those with whom he came in contact will be an inspiration for all time.

The Diamond T world-wide organization today is truly the 'lengthened shadow' of its founder and leader—our beloved 'Art' Tilt."

This "lengthened shadow" began in 1905, the year C.A. Tilt es-tablished the Diamond T Motor Car Company in Chicago, Illinois with $1,000 of capital. In 1905, the predominately-rural United States was dominated by a few large cities. One of these was Chicago, the rail center of the United States. In 1900, there were over 50,000 horse drawn vehicles, but only 377 registered automobiles with 21 registered for business use in Chicago. In fact, there were only 8,000 automobiles in the entire United States by 1906. They had access to less than 200 miles of paved roads. For most Chicagoans, walking was the most common form of transportation. Longer trips throughout Chicago were possible on the 500 mile street railway system that was fully electrified by 1906. It was in this milieu that Tilt spent eight years working in his father's business, the J.E. Tilt Shoe Company.

According to an article based on an interview with Tilt in the October 20, 1927, *Commercial Car Journal*, in 1896, at the age of nineteen, Tilt began working for his father sweeping floors. Later, he went on the road selling shoes. His father's frequent out of town business trips often left him in charge of the entire factory. His spare time was devoted to studying all aspects of automobiles.

His father sublet a machine shop to Charles Yale Knight, the inventor of the Knight Sleeve Valve engine and manufacturer of the Knight automobile. Tilt became the sales manager of the Knight Motor Car Company for about a year, from 1904 to 1905 until he left to establish Diamond T. Tilt chose "Diamond T" because it was the name his father used to distinguish the "top of the line shoes" from others offered by the company.

From 1905 to 1911 Diamond T built only passenger car chassis, sold locally with custom-built bodies. Tilt, serving "as president, general manager, salesman and chief mechanic" developed the chassis. Sources indicate that while the first Diamond T was built in 1905, it was not until 1907 that Diamond T was on the market with three body styles, a $3250 Runabout, a $3500 Touring Car, and a $4250 Limousine. A 40 HP 4-cylinder engine supplied power to the

124-inch wheelbase chassis used for all three models. These three models, with a 114-inch wheelbase, were continued in 1908, all with price increases. The Runabout, now called the Roadster, sold for $3500, the Touring Car for $4300, while the Limousine increased to $5200. In 1909, a 114-inch wheelbase Roadster was offered with a 45-50 HP engine for $2800. A 30 HP 108-inch wheelbase "Model D. 2, 3, or 4 Passenger Car" was offered in 1910 with a price range of $2250 to $3000. In 1911 Diamond T offered a $3500 "Fore Door Touring Car."

Diamond T also built its first truck in 1911, referred to as "Old No. 1." The order for the truck came from Chicago "plumbing goods" producer, L. Wolff Manufacturing Company "as a result of the exceptional service of Diamond T automobiles owned by members of the Wolff family." An early sales brochure, *Proof that Proves*, noted this order was "placed…even before a plan had been drawn or a test made." Tilt decided to discontinue automobile production in 1911. The company exhibited "commercial vehicles" at the National Automobile shows in New York in January 1912 and Chicago in February 1912. *Automobile Trade Journal*, March 1912, described the $3350 5-ton model and the $3250 3-ton model with "lighter springs." These initial models were chain driven, but by 1915, Diamond T advertised "The Most Complete Line of Worm-Driven Motor Trucks on the Market. Four models with the World's Best Units: 3/4-1 Ton…1 1/2 Ton…2 Ton…3 Ton." By 1916, various publications quoted company publicity noting that, "Diamond T trucks are to be sold in all parts of the United States, whereas in the past the Diamond T Company has confined its efforts principally to Chicago and its environs."

In 1917, Diamond T moved into new facilities, affirming the decision to concentrate on trucks and to expand marketing to "all parts of the United States." *The Automobile*, July 5, 1917 offered details. "Formal opening of what is said to be the largest factory in the world devoted exclusively to the building of motor trucks was celebrated last night [June 29] by a beefsteak dinner served in the new assembly room of the Diamond T Motor [Car] Co. C.A. Tilt, president of the company, was host to 125 guests. The new plant covers 110,000 sq.ft. and is arranged for the most progressive assembly. Production scheduled for the present calls for ten trucks a day, but there are factory facilities for turning out twenty-five to thirty a day." In a January 10, 1918, *Motor World* advertisement, Diamond T announced, "Five Sizes…Made in the Finest Truck Factory in America," and emphasized that its trucks were "The Nation's Freight Car."

America's direct involvement in World War I did not occur until 1917. However, large orders for trucks from numerous manufacturers began earlier. According to company publicity, Diamond T placed its "facilities at the disposal of the Government" starting in 1917 and built over 1400 "heavy duty 3-5 ton trucks" for the War Department. Following World War I, military orders ceased and the War Department sold its surplus vehicles to aid in the expanding efforts to improve America's highways. However, this increased supply of trucks resulted in a glut on the market. A post-war depression created further problems for Diamond T and other truck manufacturers. According to the company, Diamond T's solution to these problems was "to expand its dealer organization." The company also noted that despite adding "several hundred dealers," the "slump of 1920 hit us…. We worked hard and learned a lot before we weathered that storm, but we came through without a black mark on our record."

The 1920s

Company publicity noted that after weathering the post-war "storm," Diamond T focused on the production "of two-ton trucks and up," marketing them "largely through a factory branch organization" from 1922 to 1928. This changed in 1928, when Diamond T "decided that the day of the heavy-duty truck was nearing an end, [and] that the factory branch method of distribution was too cumbersome and expensive." *MoToR*, November 1937 summarized sales for the decade 1928 to 1937. In 1928, 88.4% of trucks sold were 2 tons or less capacity with 53.2% of sales in the 1- to 1 1/2-ton class. In 1929, 90% of the trucks sold were 2 tons or less, but the 1- to 1 1/2-ton class dropped to only 9.5% while the 1 1/2- to 2-ton class increased from 19% to 63.4%. While Diamond T officials did not know these results in 1928 they do indicate most trucks sold were light trucks. However, such a strategy put Diamond T into competition with high volume producers Chevrolet, Ford, GMC, and Dodge. Nonetheless, the result was to launch a program that "emphasized the light truck, [marketing] these trucks through a dealer rather than through a branch organization." Diamond T sold 2,308 trucks in 1928 and 3,586 in 1929, a number not exceeded until 1933. While sales increased 60 percent over 1927 and in 1929 the increase was 40 percent over 1928, Diamond T's rank only moved from 12th in 1928 to 11th in 1929 among truck manufacturers.

While Diamond T may have decided to "emphasize" light trucks, it did not abandon the heavy-duty market. For example, in 1928, Diamond T offered a 4-ton "High-Speed six-wheel model" and an 8-ton six-wheel Model 1600; and in 1929, the 3-ton Model 600. Six-cylinder Hercules engines powered these models. The lineup at the end of 1929 ranged from 1 to 12 tons and six-cylinder engines had replaced four-cylinder engines in most of the Diamond T lineup.

Truck manufacturers generally concentrated on mechanical features to sell trucks. However, increased attention to style accompanied Diamond T's emphasis on the light truck market. Advertising reflected this change. "This great new truck, Model 302, possesses two, and only two, passenger car characteristics—it is extremely fast and exceptionally good-looking." Also, "Now, more than ever, Diamond T is the 'Handsomest Truck in America.'" And, "There is no reason under the sun why a motor truck need be anything but handsome! Diamond T designers have proved that good looks can be built into good trucks." Starting in 1928, beautifully illustrated sales literature and advertisements contributed to the new image. Gone was "The Nation's Freight Car."

The 1930s

The Great Depression, signaled by the stock market crash in October 1929, was the most devastating economic crisis in United States history. From 1929 to 1933, net income from manufacturing in the United States fell by more than two-thirds. Over 86,000 businesses failed between 1930 and 1932. Average family income that had been about $2900 in 1929 was below $1600 in 1932. Diamond T's lower prices reflected these economic realities. The 1933 1 1/2-ton Model 211 sold for $595; while in 1929 the comparable 1 1/2-ton Model 290 cost $1475.

Some figures from *MoToR* will also put the impact of the Great Depression into perspective. Total truck production for the last pre-depression year, 1929, was 826,817. By 1932, generally the lowest ebb of the Great Depression, the total dropped to 245,285, a total only 29.7% of the 1929 total or a decline of 70.4%. Autocar sales were 2,939 in 1929 and only 1,015 in 1932, a 65.5% decline. Federal sold 2,851 in 1929 and 1,167 in 1932, a 59.1% decline. Mack went from 6,819 to 1,425 for a 79.2% decline. While significant, the effects of the Great Depression were not as severe for Diamond T. Sales were 3,586 in 1929 and 2,250 in 1932, a decline of 37.3%.

After 1932, Diamond T sales increased, reaching 8,750 in 1936. However, the so-called "Roosevelt Recession" of 1937-1938 was, even if only briefly, very severe with sales dropping 50% or more for most truck manufacturers. Diamond T sales declined from 8,118 in 1937 to 4,393 in 1938.

In 1935, the Diamond T Motor Car Company published *Thirty Years of Diamond-T Progress*. Given the trauma of the Great Depression, it is interesting to note the booklet's themes, later identified as C.A. Tilt's "lengthened shadow." Specifically, the success of Diamond T was the result of the stable leadership provided by its founder, who continued as President and General Manager. In addition, because of Tilt's leadership, Diamond T had never had "any reorganization or refinancing" during its entire 30 year history.

The economic difficulties of the 1930s resulted in a continued emphasis on style for Diamond T. As in the late 1920s, Diamond T offered beautiful sales brochures and advertisements. Artists exaggerated aspects of the trucks in order to give them a longer, lower, even more stylish appearance. Substance as well as style also received strong emphasis. A multi-page January 1930 *Commercial Car Journal* Diamond T advertisement devoted a page to each major component including engines, radiators, headlights, wheels, and brakes. The value conscious consumer was enticed by streamlined styling, quality components, sound engineering, mechanical substance, and lower prices. Diamond T's introduction of diesel-powered models in 1936 was clearly an example of combining cost effective mechanical features and "streamline" styling. Diamond T's 1938 and 1939 styling was even more car-like.

In fact, the 1930s is the decade that clearly identifies Diamond T as a style leader among truck manufacturers. Diamond T's emphasis on visible yearly styling changes reflected the practices of automobile manufacturers more than truck producers who generally thought primarily in terms of functionality. Planned obsolescence was not something that would directly entice a customer accustomed to seeing a truck as a long-term investment. Diamond T was hopeful that the frequently changed and upgraded Diamond Ts would expand the market and encourage increased sales.

In addition, Diamond T sought to expand its markets taking over the sales and servicing of the "Pak-Age-Car house-to-house delivery truck" in 1939. Also in 1939, Diamond T offered a "100,000 mile or one full year warranty" on all models equipped with the Super Service engines manufactured by Hercules. According to C.A. Tilt, the warranty was a reflection of "Diamond T's consistent program of engineering development."

The 1940s

A greatly expanded market did occur in the 1940s. America's entry into World War II followed the Japanese attack on Pearl Harbor, December 7, 1941. Civilian truck production continued until March 9, 1942, when the War Production Board "ordered the rationing of light, medium and heavy-duty trucks, truck-tractors and trailers." Prior to this, Diamond T began production of military vehicles. An article in the November 1941 *Commercial Car Journal* featured photographs of Diamond T "six-wheelers and armored half-tracs," as well as a wrecker, and "a tank transporter and recovery truck." In an April 1942 *Commercial Car Journal* advertisement, Diamond T announced "Diamond T Trucks. With the colors...for the duration. Diamond T will build you even finer Super Service Trucks than those which serve you today, when victory brings Peace."

According to Diamond T publicity, the company produced an as-tonishing 50,223 heavy-duty vehicles for the armed forces. This included over 31,000 six-wheel "prime movers" and 6,500 12-ton tank transporters "both designed and manufactured exclusively by Diamond T." On September 11, 1942, in a ceremony broadcast over Chicago radio station WBBM, the company received an Army-Navy "E" award "for excellence on the production front." In addition, Diamond T was awarded "several 'E' citations" for continued production excellence. Diamond T was also "authorized to build a limited number of commercial trucks for essential service" in 1944 and 1945.

Diamond T responded to the pent-up post-war demand by resuming full-scale civilian production in 1946, offering models from 1 1/2 to 10 tons capacity. C.A. Tilt resigned as President and General Manager, to become Chairman of the Board of Directors. He was succeeded by E.J Bush. Diamond T advertising material during the 1940s featured Kodachrome color photographs instead of the artist's illustrations common in the 1920s and 1930s. One such ad declared, "The older Diamond T's were great trucks. The 1946 models are even better." However, few changes were made to the post-war models. Reflecting postwar pent-up demand, sales in 1946 were 5,093, 10,475 in 1947, and 10,657 in 1948. In a harbinger of the future, however, sales declined to 5,093 in 1949. At this time, Diamond T's eleven building Chicago factory complex totaled more than 600,000 square feet.

The 1950s

The 1950s was a decade of momentous events for Diamond T. At the end of 1949 Diamond T launched its first all-new post-war models. An additional model followed in March 1950. Featuring distinctive new styling, these four 1950 models ranged from 1 1/2 to 5 tons capacity. Subsequently, Diamond T also offered a 1-ton pick-up model. Diamond T declared these new models "set completely new standards of motor truck design!" Described as "the *ultra-modern* version of 'the truck of lowest cost,'" these trucks featured cabs with a curved one-piece windshield supplied by International Harvester.

The March 1951 *Commercial Car Journal* covered the "new heavy duty line for 1951." The five new models covered the "field from

3 to 10 tons" and featured new styling including the cab used on the light-duty models previously introduced. Hercules, Continental, and Cummins diesel engines powered these trucks. In March 1952, Diamond T introduced the Cummins diesel-powered Model 950 and the Buda diesel-powered Model 951, the largest and most powerful Diamond Ts produced for commercial purposes. Additional model introductions continued throughout the 1950s. For example, in 1953, Diamond T announced a lightweight diesel, a 1 1/2-ton model, three "medium capacity" models, and an all-new Model 723 cab-over-engine (COE) tilt-cab series that added a diesel to its engine options in 1954. In 1956, a turbo-supercharged Cummins engine became an added option for the COE tilt-cab.

The Korean War (1950-1953) affected consumer production and sales. Diamond T produced trucks for the military, ending this production in 1954. During the war, Diamond T also continued to develop new models. This flurry of new models did not translate into significant sales gains. In fact, while sales in 1950 did increase to 5,675, they declined in 1951 to 4,508, to 3,420 in 1952, and 3,398 in 1953. However, these totals do not reflect orders for military trucks that exceeded civilian sales in 1952 and 1953. In 1954, military contracts associated with the Korean War ended.

E.J. Bush, Diamond T's President, addressed the company's future in his comments to shareholders in the 1954 *Annual Report*. He explained that while sales increased to 3,627 and the company's military contract ended, the 1954 loss "had more to do with the long-range programs of the independent manufacturer than current sales figures." Pointing out trends that would eventually overtake Diamond T, Bush noted, "This condition was also quite apparent in the passenger car field where several mergers were effected, and in the motor truck industry 1954 [that] saw the liquidation or sale of two independents."

Bush also took the opportunity to feature the newly introduced COE heavy-duty Tilt-Cab Model 921CN and connect it to the company's new strategy for survival. This truck would be a strategic "tool with which to increase Diamond T's percentage of the heavy-duty market," whose day Diamond T had predicted had ended back in 1928. (While never stated, perhaps the "Tilt Cab" is a kind homage to C.A. Tilt. Yes, the cab does *tilt*, but that allows the play on words.)

C.A. Tilt addressed Diamond T stockholders in the 1955 *Annual Report*. He focused on the "long-range program of shifting the emphasis of our business from a light and medium truck manufacturer to a medium and heavy-duty truck manufacturer." He noted that Diamond T's heavy-duty "business showed an increase of 94% over [1954]." This statement obscures the fact that sales of heavy duty vehicles should have increased if the company was shifting from light to heavy duty truck production. He concluded, "in spite of continuous competitive pressures in the truck industry from the volume manufacturers, we have established the fact that Diamond T can exist and profit in the commercial field without the benefit of military vehicle production."

Of great significance were Tilt's comments about the future status of the company. "Our dealer organization is also entitled to special mention for the splendid manner in which they continued their activities during the period of negotiations relative to the proposed sale of assets to the White Motor Company, with its attendant publicity. Our dealers showed the highest degree of loyalty and maintained a constant faith in the successful future of Diamond T *regardless of the element of ownership*." (Italics added.) This suggests that in the years before his death Tilt was considering the sale of Diamond T to acquisition-minded White Motor.

Also significant were the "executive changes" announced for 1956. Retirements included H. MacEvoy, with the firm since 1929; H.C. Emberson, with the company since 1917; and E.J. Bush, with Diamond T since 1919. C.A. Tilt's death on September 19, 1956, represented the most significant departure. E.J. Bush became Chairman of the Board of Directors and Zenon C.R. Hansen, President.

The 1956 *Annual Report* made no mention of possible ownership changes, focusing on the "spectacular increase in net income"—from $155,000 in 1955 to $1.3 million for 1956. The *Annual Report* declared military contracts were not essential to Diamond T's viability. "For all of the preceding seven years the profit picture had been quite unsatisfactory except when military contracts provided a substantial contribution. This condition had led many to the erroneous conclusion that government purchases were necessary for Diamond T to prosper." However, the *Annual Report* announced that Diamond T was awarded a $20 million contract to build 1,760 5-ton 6x6 military trucks, with production scheduled for 1957 and 1958. Sales actually declined from 5,111 in 1955 to 5,025 in 1956. However, the price structure of heavy duty trucks provided higher income per unit and thus greater earnings compared to "the less profitable lighter-duty line." The *Annual Report* also noted that, "It can be added that our continuing relinquishment of the light-duty field has been accompanied by an advantageous reduction in the number of our retail outlets. Some marginal dealers in the smaller communities had not the capacity and ability to merchandise and service properly the larger models which we now build."

However, like these "marginal dealers," the days of an independent, "never reorganized" Diamond T were numbered. In 1955, E.J. Bush, Diamond T's President, had emphasized the importance of the "long-range programs of the independent manufacturer." C.A. Tilt had also urged the continued faith in Diamond T's success "regardless of the element of ownership." In 1958, ownership changed and Diamond T became part of the White Motor Company. White had begun its acquisition of truck manufacturers with Sterling in 1951. Also, in 1951, while not a merger or acquisition, White completed a sales and service agreement with Freightliner. White acquired Autocar in 1953 and Reo in 1957.

The 1960s

"At Diamond T we are convinced that the 'Sixties will be Diamond T's greatest decade.' This is no hollow, chest-beating phrase. This is our sincere belief based on knowledge of what is going on at the factory, in research and development, in our experimental department and in the field. How come such prophecy when you consider Diamond T's brilliant record since 1905? The only answer is that the future must look very bright indeed. *And indeed it does.*" While surely based on "sincere belief," the prophecy was faulty. In fact, the Sixties was the last decade for Diamond T. The advertising copy from the February 1962 *Commercial Car Journal* acknowledged the significant changes occurring at Diamond T. The ad refers to the "production situation" and the "move of manufacturing." This, of course, refers to the 1960 move from the Diamond T facilities in Chicago to the Lansing, Michigan Reo factory and the creation of the Lansing Division that integrated Diamond T and Reo production. The ad also noted, "Diamond T now controls the manufacture of its own gasoline engines, sheet metal, cabs and other components formerly available only from suppliers." However, the reality behind this statement is that as a part of the White Motor Company, Diamond T used components made by other divisions. Specifically, Diamond T used cabs from Reo and Autocar and the famous 6-cylinder and V-8 Reo Gold Comet gasoline engines.

No longer free to pursue its own "long-range programs as an independent manufacturer," Diamond T had to fit into the White Motor Company's plans. Increasingly, this meant Diamond T and Reo would share components with each other as well as their corporate siblings. Examples of this strategy abound. The "D" cab, Autocar's Driver Cab introduced in 1950, showed up on Diamond T models in 1959. Diamond T models featured in the January 1960 *Commercial Car Journal* featured the "R" or Reo cab. The models in Diamond T's 1961 "D" Series were essentially Reo trucks with a Diamond T chrome bar grille. The "P" line, introduced in 1962, also featured the "R" cab, essentially the cab Reo had originally introduced in 1939. Autocar was the basis for much of Diamond T's 1000 Line "Westerner" introduced as a 1966 model. Reo's lineup included light-duty, medium-duty, and heavy-duty models that featured Autocar Driver Cabs, a 90-inch BBC model based on Diamond T's Model 990, the DCL based on the Diamond T Model 931, and the Tilt-Cab DF based on Diamond T's Model CG. In 1966, White, Diamond T, and Reo offered the Royalex-bodied Trend.

Two virtually identical truck lines resulted from all of this component sharing. White Motor Corporation's strategic plans did not include such costly duplication. While Diamond T did advertise early in the year, White introduced Diamond Reo in 1967. C.A. Tilt's "lengthened shadow" was gone.

The Diamond T Motor Car Company started in 1905. From 1905 to 1911 the company built only passenger car chassis, sold locally with custom-built bodies. Company founder C. A. Tilt developed the chassis. Models offered included chassis with roadster, touring car, and limousine bodies. Four-cylinder engines supplied power to all models. Shown above is a roadster similar to the one Tilt raced in the October 6-7, 1910 "Waukesha Run." A *Motor Age* advertisement from 1908 featured an illustration of a nearly identical model. It proclaimed the Diamond T "The Handsomest Roadster at the Show." Since the cars were sold locally, it may be the reference is to the National Automobile Show held in Chicago. The ad also noted that the Diamond T had a "Speed Capacity [of] 65 Miles an hour." In addition, "Demonstrations by Appointment" were available and the company was "Glad to Entertain visiting Agents." Photographs of Tilt in a roadster in the Waukesha Run show a car with a more rounded fender that follows the curve of the rear wheel compared to the fender of the car shown above. The Diamond T truck signs in the windows indicate Diamond T had established itself as a truck manufacturer prior to the photograph. *Eric Wentworth Collection*

Volume 1, Number 2 of the *Diamond T Compass*, June 28, 1947, the company's in-house publication, celebrated Diamond T founder C. A. Tilt's birthday. The cover featured the above photograph of "Old No. 1," the first truck built by Diamond T in 1911. According to the often-told story, the order for the truck came from the Chicago "plumbing goods" producer, L. Wolff Manufacturing Company "as a result of the exceptional service of Diamond T automobiles owned by members of the Wolff family." An early sales brochure, *Proof that Proves*, noted this order was "placed…even before a plan had been drawn or a test made." Louis Wolff's 1917 letter to Diamond T, reproduced in the brochure, said in part, "we have…the first truck built by the Diamond T Motor Car, Co. We have tried other trucks…you make no mistake in buying the Diamond T." This first truck, a "3-tonner," was chain driven. This would soon change. The *Commercial Car Journal*, March 15, 1913, told of the Diamond T's "entirely new, one-ton worm drive truck. The principal feature is the use of the new Timken worm-driven rear-axle unit." A March 22, 1919 *Literary Digest* ad noted a line up of 1- to 5-ton capacity models, and continued to use a phrase introduced in 1918: "The Diamond T truck has rightfully earned the title of 'The Nation's Freight Car,' because of its dependability—durability and its adaptability." *Detroit Public Library, National Automotive History Collection*

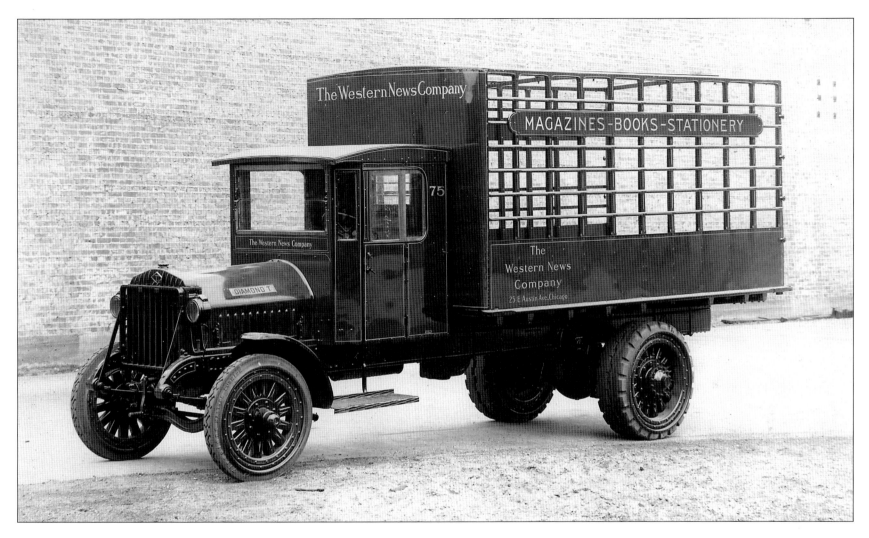

"The industrial duties of Diamond T trucks are infinite. The confectioner, as much as the steel manufacturer, has found the solution of his delivery and distribution problems in the employment of big-capacity Diamond T's. Scientific routing, maximum loading, and a transportation radius practically without limit, are possibilities and advantages common to all trucks. The added feature of ruggedness and minimum repairs, upkeep economy, and continuous hard service, are invariably the reasons advanced by Diamond T users for their complete satisfaction from its use." Diamond T introduced the 3 1/2-ton Model K in August 1920. The *Commercial Car Journal*, August 15, 1920 introductory article noted that Diamond T stressed "three principal characteristics" of the new model, "economy, power and endurance." Diamond T sales material declared the "Model K is a dividend payer and time and labor saver." A 4-cylinder 45-HP Hercules engine powered the truck. From the four-speed "transmission the power is carried to a worm-gear drive, full floating type rear axle, having a gear ratio of 8 3/4 to 1." Top speed was 12 MPH with the optional 10 1/3 to 1 gear ratio. Water circulated by means of a centrifugal pump on the motor. Cooling capacity was eight gallons. *Lon Arbegust Collection*

"You should be thoroughly satisfied that the institution standing back of the truck you purchase has a clean reputation in the industry for building a reliable product over a long period of time. In the Diamond T Motor Car Company, the men of the organization have proven their ability to build reliable, economical trucks. In addition to the continuous, experienced management of Mr. C.A. Tilt, President and General Manager of the Company, every man concerned with the construction of a Diamond T is an acknowledged truck authority…." This text from the Diamond T sales brochure for the Model T reflected the importance of the men responsible for the excellence of the Diamond T truck, in particular, the founder, C.A.Tilt. The men of the Sinclair Oil Company—Diamond T described such men as "the human element that controls the companies' destiny"—selected the 1 1/2-ton Model T shown above. A 4-cycle 22.5 HP 4-cylinder Hinkley 700 engine powered the Model T. Diamond T supplied a "Bosch High-Tension Magneto…to give extra hot spark for starting purposes." As a result, "No battery [was] necessary." The rear wheels were equipped with Duplex "double expanding" mechanical brakes. Standard equipment included side and tail oil lamps. *Lon Arbegust Collection*

In 1926, 4-cylinder engines continued to power all models offered by Diamond T. These ranged from the 3/4- to 1-ton Model 75, the 1 1/2- to 2-ton Model T3 and T4, the 2 1/2- to 3 1/2-ton Model U4, the 3 1/2- to 4-ton Model K2 shown above, and the 5- to 6-ton Model S2. Mechanical brakes, described as "Foot, expanding on rear wheels," continued to be standard on the Model K2. A mechanical hand brake also operated on the rear wheels only. Diamond T offered 170- and 180-inch wheelbases for the basic 8,020-pound chassis. A 3-main bearing Hercules LA engine that developed 32.4 HP (N.A.C.C. rating) powered this worm-drive truck. A full-floating rear axle was standard. Pneumatic tires, while increasingly popular with lighter capacity models, were not standard on this model, due to concerns about overloading—a common habit of many operators of heavy-duty models—and tire failure. The light-duty Reo Speed Wagon, introduced in 1915, featured pneumatic tires as standard. Wheels were cast steel. A set of "tools, jack, hubodometer, electric tail lamp, electric headlights, front bumper, front fenders and horn" were standard on the Model K2. The electrical system featured a "high tension magneto." Diamond T supplied a four-speed "selective-sliding" transmission. *Lon Arbegust Collection*

"A new model, known as Special Delivery Model 75 has been added to the Diamond T truck line. The truck is designed for high speed light delivery work and serves as a compliment to the [Diamond T] line of heavier models." *Motor World*, December 20, 1923 covered Diamond T's response to the Reo Speed Wagon, introduced in 1915. The Reo Speed Wagon was equipped with shaft drive, an electric starter and lights, and pneumatic tires. *Commercial Car Journal* referred to this class of trucks as "Speed Trucks," the term used by the industry since Reo had trademarked "Speed Wagon." Like the Reo Speed Wagon, the 130-inch wheelbase Diamond T Model 75 had a 3/4-ton capacity. A.O. Smith Corporation supplied the frame. By 1926, *Motor Age* reported that Diamond T exhibited a new one-ton capacity Model 76 at the "delivery truck show held at the Sherman, Chicago, Feb. 1 to 6." The Dugan Brothers fleet, shown above, consisted of seventeen Model 76 delivery trucks. A 4-cylinder 25.6 HP Hercules OXA engine continued to supply the power for the 130-inch wheelbase model. Diamond T selected front and rear Columbia axles, manufactured by Columbia Axle, Company, Cleveland, Ohio for the Model 76. Driver access was limited to the right side on the vehicles shown as indicated by the spare tire location. *Lon Arbegust Collection*

"In designing the new model 76 fast 1-tonner, Diamond T has made not only a strong bid for light delivery business but has put into practice its new policy of designing a truck that is as pleasing to the eye as a private car." Heralding this new design focus, *Automotive Industries*, February 4, 1926 continued, "An aluminum radiator shell, with a cellular core, Biflex bumper and hollow-spoke steel wheels carrying 30 x 5 in. pneumatic tires give it a de luxe finish." The quality of the components used by Diamond T was an important advertising focus. According to a Diamond T and G & O Manufacturing Company advertisement, "Located as they are, near the very centre of the automotive industry, Diamond T could choose any one of a number of radiators—and save thereby. But Diamond T goes to New Haven, 1000 miles away, to get a better radiator. G & O Radiators cost more to make than many others—and cost Diamond T more. But it's an investment that pays well, in the form of an almost total absence of radiator service expense to Diamond T owners and dealers." In 1926, Diamond T competed with 45 manufacturers in the 1-ton field. *Lon Arbegust Collection*

"Diamond T Trucks have quality and unimpeachable records of performance. Their appearance has an advertising value to owners. The line is complete—a truck for every need. These with reasonable price, personal selling helps, highest class printed selling aids, a direct mail campaign furnished, exceptional discounts and retail payment plan without finance charge—mean *you make money. Investigate.*" While this August 20, 1927 *Commercial Car Journal* ad copy was aimed at potential dealers, it reveals the importance of appearance and performance Diamond T wanted its dealers to communicate to potential customers. This fleet of five Diamond Ts indicates a dealer successfully communicated and convinced the Simmons Company. C.A. Tilt, President of Diamond T, was often the focus of company advertising and sales material. In a 1927 brochure his photograph accompanies this text: "The simplest mechanism is always the best. For instance, if we could build a motor truck with one cylinder and one moving part, and this mechanism would do the work of the present day truck, it would of course be adopted. The only thing that counts in hauling freight is cost." However, Diamond T also emphasized style. Referring to the cab shown above, Diamond T declared it "presents [a] graceful and powerful appearance in addition to its unmatched utility." *Lon Arbegust Collection*

"Massively built and rugged as it appears to the eye, this 3 1/2-ton model, one of the 'Giants of the Line,' has the benefits of the most scientific designing and assembly to prevent massiveness from becoming excess weight. This logically accounts for Diamond T's long service life. A clean-cut, flexible, and sturdy heavy duty truck is this model K." Diamond T's promotion also noted, "We have foreseen that lack of lubrication is the gravest danger a truck has to face. Therefore Model K has been equipped with the Alemite Lubricating System, which forces grease between bearing surfaces." The "powerful" four-cylinder 45 HP engine was "cradled in the frame by means of a five-inch trunnion arm in front and by 'everyway motion' supports at each side in the rear." In addition to the standard 170-inch length version shown above, Diamond T offered optional wheelbase lengths of 160 to 200 inches for the 7,250-pound chassis model. Front and rear tracks measured 66 1/4 and 65 1/4 inches respectively. The worm gear drive Model K featured a "four speeds forward and reverse transmission." Top speed was 12 MPH with 10 1/3 gear ratio. Owner William Richert, Cicero, Illinois installed a block and tackle system, anchored to the front of the frame, to load and unload cargo. *Lon Arbegust Collection*

Diamond T's 1927 lineup of eleven vehicles featured this 2 1/2-ton Model U4. The 163-inch wheelbase model had a 6100-pound chassis weight with standard 36 x 4 solid front and 38 x 8 solid rear tires. A 28.9 HP (N.A.C.C. rated) Hercules KA engine powered the Pierce governor-equipped Model U4. A Timken 6566 worm drive rear axle and a Timken 1544B front axle were standard. At one point, all Diamond Ts were equipped with worm drive rear axles. Diamond T sales material asserted "this type costs a little more than some other kinds, but that's because it is better. It has the fewest parts, just the worm wheel and the worm gear. A worm drive has more teeth in mesh at all times than any other drive… thereby reducing the percentage of lost power." Among the components touted by Diamond T were Titeflex fuel and vacuum lines. As advertising noted "Vibration, road shock, and the movement of chassis units, cause fuel lines of solid metal tubing to crystallize and break. Titeflex lines absorb vibration…never crystallize. They are all-metal and being flexible, are easily installed [and] speed up production. They are liquid-tight and air-tight, and remain so." Rear wheel mechanical brakes continued to be used on the 1927 models. Diamond T adopted hydraulic brakes in 1928. *Lon Arbegust Collection*

"Ungoverned Power destroys Even the Most Rugged Machine. For safe, Economical Operation 'Diamond T' Trucks Are PIERCE protected! Power protection assures more dependable service, longer life, freedom from accidents caused by speeding, fewer repair bills, and lower operating costs. That's why leading manufacturers such as 'Diamond T' have adopted [the] dependable PIERCE GOVERNOR as standard equipment." Pierce governors, manufactured in Anderson, Indiana, limited the "engine against racing and vibration." Pierce argued that preventing "excessive speed" reduced accidents, saved tires, and reduced repair and operating costs. A Pierce governor was standard on this 1927 Diamond T. Diamond T equipped its 1927 models with mechanical Duplex rear wheel brakes. The shorter hood and single set of hood louvers on the model shown above indicates an earlier in the year model. Changes to come later in 1927 would include a longer hood, two sets of horizontal hood louvers, and a cab featuring a flatter roof. Diamond T emphasized the 650-pound "full open, half door or full vestibule steel cab" was "ingeniously mounted with rubber cushions to offset the racking, twisting, and weaving due to uneven roads." The cab also presented a "graceful and powerful appearance in addition to its unmatched utility." *Lon Arbegust Collection*

"Motor Trucks of Quality" was a slogan used for a series of Diamond T advertisements in 1927 and 1928. These ads also initiated the practice of distorting the truck's proportions to enhance its appearance, in particular, a lowered cab and hood height and lengthened hood. This was a practice used extensively until photography became the medium of choice for Diamond T in the 1940s. Typical of the advertising copy is this from July 1927: "You should see the new Diamond T trucks with powerful, dependable six-cylinder engines, four wheel hydraulic brakes, *truck* units throughout and remarkable beauty in appearance." It is interesting to note that the monthly *Commercial Car Journal* specifications do not list a Diamond T model with a six-cylinder engine in 1927. *Automotive Industries* did announce new 6-cylinder models in the February 11, 1928 and February 28, 1928 issues. The trucks shown above and on the following page are probably 2 1/2-ton Model U4s. According to the *Commercial Car Journal*, a 4-cylinder 28.9 HP (N.A.C.C. rated) Hercules KA engine supplied the power to this model. The brakes were located on the rear wheels only. During 1927, the two rows of horizontal hood louvers shown above replaced the single set of vertical louvers used on earlier models. *Lon Arbegust Collection*

23

In a *Commercial Car Journal*, October 20, 1927 ad, the Pyramids of Egypt are the background for a line of three Diamond T trucks. The text exclaims "STABILITY. Fleet owners now know what their cost records reveal. Comparative figures show DIAMOND T TRUCKS most economical to operate and maintain. DIAMOND T TRUCKS are built on a principle as sound as the pyramids. Many large fleet owners have standardized on DIAMOND T TRUCKS, manufactured by a company whose stability is unquestioned and a company which never has been refinanced or reorganized." The point: Diamond T as a truck and as a company is as solid and stable and as durable as the pyramids. One of the "stable" trucks featured was similar to the model shown above. Information identifying the specific model was not included with the photograph. In all probability it is a 2 1/2-ton Model U4. According to *Commercial Car Journal* specifications, Diamond T offered only 4-cylinder engines in 1927. The advertisement also noted that Diamond Ts were *"First in Appearance and Quality,"* indicating the ever-increasing emphasis on styling leadership and the continuation of high quality and economical operation and maintenance. The redesigned bumper and radiator shroud are a reflection of this philosophy. *Lon Arbegust Collection*

"Diamond T, builder of fine motor trucks for nearly a quarter of a century again signalizes its engineering leadership of the motor truck industry." This text was part of the 1928 sales brochure introducing the new 6-cylinder models. The brochure prominently featured full color paintings illustrating each model. Shown in vivid reds and greens—Diamond T's signature colors—the styling was the center of attention. "Here are trucks new in style—lower, smarter, with more snap, and life. Diamond T pioneered good looks in good trucks.... Why should a truck have to be clumsy, stodgy, awkward? Diamond T proved long ago that such ugliness was unnecessary." Referring to the new trucks as "The Handsomest Trucks in America," Diamond T declared, "These good-looking carriers stamp their owners as progressive, wide-awake firms." A "Diamond T heavy-duty" 6-cylinder 74 HP Hercules engine supplied the power to the 128 1/2-inch wheelbase 2 1/2-ton Model 550 tractor, shown above. The truck featured a 6 1/2- x 3- x 1/4-inch "extra heavy heat treated chrome nickel steel frame." A 4-speed transmission allowed the tractor to reach a 30 MPH top speed. Four-wheel Lockheed hydraulic brakes with a "special vacuum booster" were standard and controlled "these Diamond T's with velvet ease, even under full load." *Detroit Public Library, National Automotive History Collection*

Automobile Topics, July 28, 1928 introduced the new Diamond T 2-ton Model 400 and the 2 1/2-ton Model 502 and featured a photograph of a chassis only version of the Model 400 shown above. *Automotive Industries,* August 4, 1928 offered details about the new models. "Both models are powered by six-cylinder engines, have Lockheed hydraulic four wheel brakes, cam and lever steering gear and other features designed to give long service and easy handling." A 66 HP 6-cylinder Hercules WXB powered the Model 400. A larger 74.5 HP Hercules engine powered the Model 502. "Both engines have seven bearing camshafts; molybdenum steel wrist pins 1 1/8 in. in diameter; cast iron pistons with four rings; pressure lubrication by means of a gear type pump to main and connecting rod bearings; Filtrator oil purifier; Zenith carburetor; air cleaner and governor, [and] Clark front and rear axles. The standard wheelbase for the 2-ton [Model 400] is 163 in. Two wheelbases of 163 and 17 in. are available in the larger [Model 502]. Optional wheelbases at extra cost range from 141 1/2 to 188 in." Spiral bevel drive was featured. Budd steel disk wheels were standard equipment. Solid tires and single rear tires required the steel-spoke wheels as shown. *Lon Arbegust Collection*

"Motor Trucks of Quality. It is easier to sell Diamond T trucks than to sell against them." In 1927 and 1928, Diamond T ran a series of 2-page advertisements that featured gold and red or green color schemes, artist's illustrations, and these slogans. Diamond T introduced the six-wheel four-wheel-drive 4-ton Model 800 in 1928 and featured it in some of these advertisements. According to *Automotive Industries*, August 11, 1928, "Rubber blocks as a means of absorbing torque differences between the two driving axles, and to allow a trailing action by the front pair of driving wheels in rounding turns" were incorporated into the rear axle linkage. The two Timken "heavy-duty" rear axles were "connected together by two rocker beams which are anchored to the axles by heavy fin plates." A 6-cylinder 93.5 HP "Diamond T Hercules" YXC engine powered the Model 800. The steel cab, "impressive in appearance and unequaled for comfort of the driver," featured flexible three-point mounting to the frame. According to sales literature, "the cab can be used either as a full open, half door, or full vestibule cab to suit all weather conditions." Lockheed hydraulic brakes on the four rear wheels featured 3 1/2-inch wide 16-inch drums. Five wheelbase options were available ranging from 176 1/4 to 215 3/8 inches. *Detroit Public Library, National Automotive History Collection*

"Now, more than ever, Diamond T is 'the Handsomest Truck in America.' Your motor truck is your moving billboard. Its appearance, good or bad, reflects your business standards. Long ago Diamond T pioneered good looks in trucks. From its smartly nickeled radiator to its distinctive wheels, beautiful low slung bodies and sedan-like cab interiors, Model 302 [shown above] is modern as this morning's newspaper." Gone is "The Nation's Freight Car" slogan. However, Diamond T sought to reassure the customer that beauty was more than skin deep. "This great new truck…possesses two, and only two, passenger car characteristics—it is extremely fast and exceptionally good looking. There passenger car influence ends abruptly. From its magnificently powerful 7-bearing motor, down to its smallest forging, it is *every inch a truck*." Specifically, a 66-HP 6-cylinder Hercules WXB powered this model. The 6 1/2- x 3- x 1/4-inch "pressed steel frame" was "carefully designed with channel cross members to absorb and dissipate distortion due to uneven loads." The Model 302 was equipped with a "drop-forged I-beam construction [front axle with] Timken bearings in hub and steering pivots." The semi-floating type spiral bevel drive rear axle featured a cast steel housing. The four-speed transmission, "designed for heavy duty and severe operating conditions" was "subject to thirteen different heat-treating operations." *Detroit Public Library, National Automotive History Collection*

"Neither words nor pictures ever put quality into a motor truck—ever gave it a single virtue which its engineers had overlooked…. But in all seriousness, and with a quarter-century's reputation at stake, Diamond T makes this plain, understandable statement of fact, and asks you to convince yourself of the truth of it by actual eyesight inspection of the truck itself." "Eyesight inspection" of this model reveals a modified cab. Not as deep as the standard steel cab that was designed "as a full open, half door, or full vestibule cab," it featured opera windows and a two-piece angled windshield with triangular side glass. The windshield, mounted further forward than the standard cab allowed for a roomier interior and an opportunity to provide additional payload with a longer body. Diamond T also provided a unique frame. It featured "special construction with kick-up over [the] rear axle to provide a very low body platform. With normal load frame height is 25 inches above street level. Strength without excessive weight provided by heat treated chrome nickel steel, die formed and of ample section. Fully reinforced with cross members and gusset plates. Channel section 6 1/2 inches, width of flange 3 inches, thickness of material 1/4 inch." *Lon Arbegust Collection*

In August 1929, Diamond T introduced the 8-ton Model 1600. According to *Automotive Industries*, September 7, 1929, "the rear axle bogey is of Timken design and manufacture, whereas the rear axles in the Model 800 were Diamond T's own design." The Timken SW-300 bogey featured worm drive in both axles "without the use of an intermediate differential. Both *Automotive Industries* and *Commercial Car Journal* used the above photograph, supplied by Diamond T, in their coverage of the new model to illustrate the "flexibility of the Timken SW bogey." The 9- x 3 3/4- x 1/4-inch frame, constructed of heat-treated chrome-nickel steel, featured six cross members and "heavy steel plates, ranging from 9 to 14 inches in width…riveted to the side rails." In 1930, the International Nickel Company (INCO) featured a photograph of the Model 1600 in an advertisement. The ad noted the "widespread use of Nickel Alloy Steels for highly stressed parts of heavy duty trucks, buses and tractors, is evidence that they provide a combination of toughness, wear resistance, fatigue and impact-resistance." The Model 1600 featured a Brown-Lipe "70" seven forward and 4 reverse speed transmission that also used nickel steel for gears and shafts. *Detroit Public Library, National Automotive History Collection*

"Six wheels—four drive. A revelation of hauling efficiency is announced by the Diamond T Motor Car Company in the new Diamond T six-wheel truck. Four wheels drive and four wheels brake." A 6-cylinder 106 HP seven main bearing Hercules XXC-2 engine powered the Model 1600, shown above. *Commercial Car Journal* noted the truck was governed to operate at a maximum speed of 25 MPH with a 9 1/3 to 1 axle ratio, but could be increased to 35 MPH with an optional 7 1/4 to 1 axle ratio. Governed down the engine developed 98 HP. The radiator core, "specially designed for Diamond T," was "of the copper fin and crimped flat tube type." It was "practically burst-proof due to the ability of the flat tube to expand if the water freezes. The shell, built up of four castings was spring mounted on the frame." Later models featured angled tubes. The six-wheel truck featured Ross cam and lever steering with "a special double mounting lug which insures rigidity and extra strength." The truck featured alloy steel semi-elliptical front springs with 11 leaves that were 3 inches wide and 46 inches long. The semi-elliptical rear springs had seventeen 4-inch wide and 50-inch long leaves. *Detroit Public Library, National Automotive History Collection*

By 1930, Diamond T offered Westinghouse Automotive Air Brakes as standard equipment on all six-wheel models. Westinghouse featured a Diamond T "tank truck" similar to the model shown in a February 1930 *Commercial Car Journal* advertisement. "By permitting faster running speeds and swift, easy handling through traffic clogged areas, Westinghouse control has become an important economic feature of today's highway transport systems." The Westinghouse ad spoke to the issue of safety related to the increasingly larger capacity trucks offered by Diamond T as well as other manufacturers: "Fleet operators are no longer content with slow, uncertain brakes that make the heavy duty vehicle a liability instead of an asset." As a result, "Westinghouse Automotive Air Brakes give the modern commercial vehicle the quick, effortless stopping ability that perfectly balances modern speed, power and hauling capacity." Diamond T's 1930 models featured new styling as well. *Commercial Car Journal* described the new styling in May 1930. "Custom-built appearance has been attained by streamlining hood and cab, use of a new type chromium-plated radiator and long sweeping fenders which are carried back to the end of the cowl." The streamlined hood featured "modern rectangular" louvers, "in vogue in passenger car design." *Detroit Public Library, National Automotive History Collection*

"Forging Ahead On Spoksteels. Above the wheel-line the chassis is built like a freight car—that is what Standard Forging Company requires. It needs something more—sturdy wheels under a chassis that take any load and *like it*—that means Spoksteel." The photograph of the Model 1600 shown above was featured in the Motor Wheel Corporation advertisement quoted. The comparison to a chassis "built like a freight car" is reminiscent of Diamond T's slogan "The Nation's Freight Car." Motor Wheel, located in Lansing, Michigan, extolled the virtues of its wheel in additional ad copy: "The spider is forged from a single piece of high carbon steel for strength combined with lightness. Cooling is continuous, through fan-action of spokes. Locking is positive because of the swivel lock nut and cone originated by Spoksteel." The 190-inch standard wheelbase chassis weighed approximately 11,700 pounds, while the cab added 670 pounds. Model 1600 standard equipment included "heavy front fenders, grooved floor boards, speedometer, electric head and tail lights, starter, generator, battery, bumper, set of tools, jack, horn and thermostats." The introductory base price in 1929 had been $7500. By March 1930, the 4-ton Model 801 was $4140, the 8-ton 1600 was $6220 and the 8-ton Model 1601 was $7500. A 10-12-ton Model 2500 was now in the lineup with a base price of $8000. For comparison, Diamond T's least expensive offering, the 1-ton Model 200 was only $785.
Detroit Public Library, National Automotive History Collection

The six-ton Model 1200, shown above, was a unique design offered by Diamond T. The "graceful and powerful" steel cab was "especially designed for this model" and integrated into the body. Boyd Transfer Company, Minneapolis, Minnesota also specified a radiator shroud that differed from the standard Diamond T design. The body often referred to as a moving van, suited businesses that could utilize the over-the-cab cargo space. Based on the six-wheel models first introduced in 1928, the Model 1200 featured a 9- x 3 1/4- x 1/4-inch "heat treated chrome nickel steel" frame utilizing six cross members for added strength. Diamond T emphasized the "heat-treated chrome nickel steel" rear transmission cross member. The front transmission cross member, "an exclusive Diamond T feature," permitted "easy accessibility to [the] transmission." The semi-elliptical front springs consisted of ten leaves 3 inches wide and 46 inches long. The rear springs consisted of 15 leaves 4 x 50 inches long. Diamond T emphasized, "No pins or shackles are used on [the] rear springs—they operate only to cushion the load, which is carried to the springs through steel bearing blocks of special Diamond T design. No lubrication is necessary." Five wheelbase options ranged from 174 1/2 to 210 inches. *Detroit Public Library, National Automotive History Collection*

The "Diamond T Model 151 is genuinely a *Truck of Today*. In sturdiness, in trigger-quick performance, in downright handsomeness, it is built to be part of today's swift and colorful traffic. This great Diamond T 1-ton SIX is ALL truck. Model 151 is not to be confused with the common so-called one-ton converted passenger car unit. It is a TRUCK—a Diamond T—built by pioneer truck builders." As this quote indicates, 1929 Diamond T sales literature sought to promote style *and* substance. This emphasis was particularly true of the De Luxe cabs built to "provide sedan comfort and convenience in all weather. Crystal plate glass of three-sixteenths inch thickness runs in deep felt and rubber channels, and is provided with quick-lift cranks. Steel inside door panels. Switch, ammeter, oil gauge, heat indicator and speedometer grouped in handsome panel. Long, handy gearshift and brake levers. Easy-grip 18-inch steering wheel with polished aluminum spider. Heavily nickeled, graceful saddle lamp brackets and lamp at cowl." In addition "drip mouldings and a cadet visor protect the windows and windshield." A 61 HP 214.7-ci 6-cylinder Continental engine powered the Model 151. Diamond T supplied a three-speed transmission, Spicer "all-metal universal joints," and four wheel Lockheed hydraulic brakes. "Reinforced with channel cross members," the "pressed steel frame measured 5 x 3 x 3/16 inches." *Detroit Public Library, National Automotive History Collection*

In 1930, Diamond T celebrated its silver anniversary. The deepening effects of the Great Depression tempered the celebration. Price was becoming increasingly important. *Power Wagon*, May 1930 announced, "Motor truck users of smaller capacity delivery units priced at figures below $1000 will be interested in the announcement of an entirely new 1-ton Model 200 by the Diamond T Motor Car Company. Model 200 is a four-cylinder, heavy-duty truck priced at $785, chassis at the factory. As a companion to the new Model 200, Diamond T has also announced a 1-ton six cylinder truck the new Model 215, priced at $885." *Commercial Car Journal* covered the new models in January 1930. The photograph in the article featured the new models and noted, "Horizontal louvers distinguish the new 1-ton models." Later in the model year, the four rectangular louvers, as shown above on the hood sides, became standard. Buda engines powered both models with a 45 HP 4-cylinder engine in the Model 200 and a 48 HP 6-cylinder engine in the Model 215. According to Diamond T, the new models "look their handsomest with the famous Diamond T De Luxe Cab, especially designed to harmonize in lines with cowl, hood and radiator." *Detroit Public Library, National Automotive History Collection*

Quality components were a source of pride for Diamond T. A multi-page January 1930 *Commercial Car Journal* advertisement featured some used on the Model 200 shown above. "Dayton: The Mark of a Good Wheel." Diamond T featured Dayton Steel Wheels, shown above, on many models equipped with pneumatic tires. According to the ad there were ten "definite advantages" for Dayton Steel wheels including "Cast in one piece from the highest grade electric furnace steel." Also, "PERFECT ALIGNMENT, utmost ventilation, ample clearance between tires, a minimum of parts, easily accessible, and profitable speed—better traction—more payloads—longer truck life." Emergency brakes were another featured component. "There was a time when drivers didn't expect much of an emergency brake…and they we seldom disappointed. That was before Tru-Stop made the emergency brake mean just that…. Tru-Stop is a ventilated disc of forged steel which spins between shoes faced with the finest moulded lining." American Cable Company Inc., Bridgeport, Connecticut manufactured Tru-Stop brakes. Various models featured Auto-Lite starting motors. "Quality materials, fine workmanship and absolute reliability won Diamond T to Auto-Lite in 1925, and have firmly held this quality builder's business since." The Electric Auto-Lite Company was located in Toledo, Ohio. *Detroit Public Library, National Automotive History Collection*

"There is one way only in which Diamond T motor trucks are built. Diamond T engineers and Diamond T craftsmen, specialists in heavy-duty, *quality* motor trucks, have never built any other kind. It is doubtful if they would know how." While not identified, the truck featured above is probably the 6-cylinder one-ton Model 215. It featured a 135 1/8-inch wheelbase, 6 inches longer than the 4-cylinder Model 200. The extra length accommodated the larger 6-cylinder 214.7-ci 48 HP seven main bearing Buda engine. According to the January 1930 *Commercial Car Journal* multi-page advertisement, the R.E. Dietz Company supplied headlights for Diamond T. The ad noted "Today, as ninety years ago, the name of Dietz means the best light to drive by. Dietz lanterns and lights were famous 'way back in Andrew Jackson's time.' Dietz Twilite Headlamps are today the only fixed focus type of headlamps that have the official approval of state Motor Vehicle Departments." Diamond T sales literature touted the "Sturdy Frame Construction" of the Model 215. "Frame construction is uncommonly sturdy for a truck of one-ton rating. The tapered frame is six inches deep at the point of greatest stress, with a two and one-half inch flange. Four cross members are used, the two center members being of the high efficiency alligator-jaw type." *Detroit Public Library, National Automotive History Collection*

"To Diamond T alone goes the credit for forcing the truck industry to produce better looking trucks. But Diamond T did not rest. Today Diamond T style is further ahead than ever." The *Commercial Car Journal*, May 1930 reflected this theme in its coverage of the 2-ton Model 303 shown above. "Diamond T makes line still better looking. Designed in modern truck style, Diamond T Model 303, typical of the current production, embodies a new De Luxe cab, streamlined to conform to the hood, chromium-plated radiator, four rectangular louvers in hood sides and unusually long fenders." A 66 HP 6-cylinder seven bearing Hercules-built engine supplied the power. According to the January 1930 *Commercial Car Journal* Diamond T advertisement, these Hercules engines provided "*The* Stoutest Heart a truck could have." These engines featured "full water jacketing of combustion and valve areas, extra large water passages and high velocity pump, and force-feed lubrication to all main and connecting rod bearings." The Model 303 featured a Covert 4-speed transmission. "The name of Covert on a truck transmission case means the builder of that truck has gone all the way toward insuring efficient, enduring transmission of power in his product." Diamond T also equipped the Model 303 with five-leaf helper springs. *Detroit Public Library, National Automotive History Collection*

"There is a Diamond T for every use to which a truck is put…they vary in hauling capacity from 1 to 12 tons; they vary in type—bevel drive, worm drive and six wheel dual worm drive; they vary in character—high speed models, medium speed heavy duty models, extra heavy duty models of tremendous power and traction. But there is one very important respect in which for 25 years, Diamond T trucks have never been allowed to vary in the slightest degree…that is quality!" As a result of Diamond T's use of Timken axles, the Timken-Detroit Axle Company devoted a page to Diamond T's extensive January 1930 *Commercial Car Journal* advertisement. The advertisement declared "The employment of Timken Axles by a truck manufacturer implies—indeed insures—that he values dependability and owner-economy more than low factory cost. Timken axles thus become more than a specification…they become a symbol of the builder's clear-eyed understanding of his obligation to those who buy his motor truck." Diamond T used full floating axles, whether bevel gear or worm drive, in all models. Interestingly, the fleet of 1-ton Model 200s shown above features the older style headlights and the newer rectangular hood louvers. *Detroit Public Library, National Automotive History Collection*

"Diamond T is presenting as a leader in its line for 1932 a new low priced 1 1/2 ton six cylinder truck." Erroneously listed as $795, instead of $595, the price was "by far the lowest ever placed upon a Diamond T truck and is directly in the highly competitive low-price bracket of one and one-half tonners." In addition to this text, *Commercial Car Journal*, May 1932, used the photograph shown above. A 6-cylinder 7-bearing 228-ci 60 HP Hercules JXA engine powered the new Model 210. According to *Commercial Car Journal*, the "Rear axle is a full floating spiral bevel Clark B 373 E, with straddle mounted pinion. [The] wheel bearings are centered directly above road contact even with dual rear wheels. Timken roller bearings at differential and wheel hubs." The transmission was a 4-speed Warner Gear T9. Four-wheel Lockheed hydraulic brakes were standard. In the June *Commercial Car Journal* the price of the Model 210 was corrected and listed at $595 with the Model 240 at $795. The Model 210 shown above featured the optional 158-inch wheelbase and dual rear tires. The standard 135-inch wheelbase handled bodies up to 9 feet in length while the 158-inch wheelbase accommodated up to 11-foot long bodies. Four-leaf helper springs were optional. *Detroit Public Library, National Automotive History Collection*

Later in 1932, Diamond T offered two variations of the Model 210 shown above. The SF featured a "Semi-floating spiral bevel axle of massive construction with one-piece housing cast of electric furnace steel. Pinion straddle mounted on three rows of bearings. Double Timken roller bearings at [the] wheels." The FF featured "[a] heavy-duty spiral bevel [axle]. Full-floating design with double Timken wheel bearings centered directly above [the] tires." The 6-cylinder 60 HP Diamond T Hurricane Six supplied by Hercules powered both the Model 210SF and 210FF. The $545 and $565 "chassis at factory prices" for the SF and FF respectively reflected the lowest point of the Great Depression in the fall of 1932. These Model 210s featured the "new Diamond T steel cab, impressive in appearance and unequaled for comfort for the driver." In advertising illustrations, distorted cab and hood proportions gave the truck a lower and longer profile, in particular, the height of the upper portion of the cab. As a means to increase business during the Depression, Diamond T manufactured bodies. Available for mounting on a Diamond T chassis was a $375 "enclosed body" and a $185 10-foot stake body, designed for general hauling purposes. "All hardware is wrought iron and no castings or malleables are employed." *Detroit Public Library, National Automotive History Collection*

According to Diamond T publicity, the Schlitz Brewing Company operated a "large fleet" of Diamond T trucks. Initially, a 6-cylinder 298-ci 69 HP Hercules WXB engine powered the 3-ton Model 410. Later this engine was replaced with a 6-cylinder 339-ci 95 HP Hercules WXB. The Model 410 was part of Diamond T's "five-model low price line" that also included the 210, 240A, 310, and 510. The Model 410 featured a 6 1/2- x 3- x 1/4-inch frame made of "heat treated chrome nickel steel—the toughest and strongest frame material obtainable." "Heavy steel fishplate" was also used. The front springs consisted of ten leaves and measured 2 1/2 x 45 1/4 inches. The 3- x 56-inch rear springs consisted of 14 leaves. Six-leaf helper springs were available. Hotchkiss drive was standard with radius rods "optional at slight extra cost." A five-speed transmission was standard. Prohibition would end in December 1933, but prior to that Congress passed legislation making 3.2% beer non-intoxicating and taxing it. As a result, breweries started to produce beer since it did not violate the Nineteenth Amendment. Consequently, trucks could deliver beer to a "thirsty" public prior to December 1933. The "Beer Bodies" were an effort to meet this new demand. *Detroit Public Library, National Automotive History Collection*

This standard Model 210 was equipped with a "drop-skirt enclosed body." This body differed from the Enclosed Beer Body No. 28. Lower at the top, it was flush with the cab roof. At the bottom it was flush with the running board instead of the bottom of the cab door. The Beer Bodies design was based on the standard beer case of the day: 19 1/4 x 12 x 10 1/4 inches. Diamond T collaborated with a "number of the largest brewers and beer distributors" in the design of these bodies. The "floor, frame, sills and cross-bows are of seasoned oak with hickory crossmembers reinforced with iron." All of the "doors lock when slammed shut and open only by key carried by driver." The wheel housings are "finished square n the inside to the exact size of two cases and facilitate loading." To provide a smooth ride, the front and rear springs were carried in compression type rubber bushings, eliminating 12 lubrication points from traditional mounting systems. The 42- x 2-inch front springs were shackled at the front to reduce "shimmy." The 50- x 2 1/2-inch rear springs consisted of nine leaves. The crank operated windshield maximized airflow in the pre-air conditioning days. *Detroit Public Library, National Automotive History Collection*

Diamond T's advertising highlighted the 1933 Model 211's "striking and brilliant style," noting the "sweeping lines, flowing from the wide, drop-center bumper and Vee radiator guard, terminate in deeply skirted fenders. The new Diamond T De Luxe Cab received particular emphasis. It featured a "stream-lined Vee windshield with the panes framed in chromium." Not all Diamond T customers needed the "stream-lined Vee windshield" of a DeLuxe Cab. While the Riverside Dairy selected a unique delivery body for their Model 211SF, they still got the new "streamlined" styling of the radiator, fenders, and bumper. Diamond T used "beautiful" to describe aspects of the trucks design. It is not often that "beautiful" is associated with truck design. While not beautiful, Diamond T also promoted key engineering features. "The famous Diamond T engine is without doubt the finest truck engine ever developed in America. It has deliberately been built large enough to handle the biggest jobs with ease." Diamond T was describing the 6-cylinder 228-ci 63 HP 7-bearing Hercules JXA engine that powered the 1933 Model 211. The Model 211 offered two rear axle options. The SF featured a semi-floating spiral bevel axle "of massive construction" designed for trucks with single tires. The FF, for dual wheels, featured full-floating spiral bevel axles. *Lon Arbegust Collection*

"Diamond T Designs a Completely Stream-lined Tank Truck" was the headline for the *Commercial Car Journal*, December 1933 coverage of this radically streamlined Diamond T. The article noted "Taking advantage of the fact that liquids, unlike other loads carried by trucks, impose no limitations upon the shape of the container in which they are carried, the Diamond T Motor Car Co. and the Texas Co. have designed a 1500 gal. tank truck of unusual design and construction." The truck had a 140-inch wheelbase and weight distribution of "45 per cent on the front axle and 55 per cent on the rear." Overall length was 26 feet, width 92 inches, and a loaded height of only 79 inches. *Business Week*, December 2, 1933 labeled it the "Biggest Tortoise," declaring, "There has been a lot of talk, mostly sales-talk, about streamlined automobiles…, but the first honestly streamlined vehicle (for immediate commercial use) is not a passenger car, but a truck." According to *Commercial Car Journal*, "The engine is mounted longitudinally in the rear tail compartment with the radiator mounted cross-wise behind the oil storage tanks. A top section of the tail housing opens to permit a mechanic to stand erect as he works on the engine." All controls including the brakes, horn, clutch, transmission, and steering were air operated. *Detroit Public Library, National Automotive History Collection*

"Proved performance leadership! Founded 28 years ago, Diamond T builds nothing but trucks. For years Diamond T has been the preferred truck of scores of the nation's leading corporations and largest truck users, operating fleets of as many as 3,000 Diamond T trucks!" Diamond T's emphasis on style was always matched by its emphasis on its engineering quality and reliability. Sales material for the 1933 Model 211 offered these points. "Here is style unmatched in the entire truck field—style as far advanced over ordinary truck standards as [is] the mechanical construction and the performance." For example, "The hollow spoke metal wheel has tremendous strength and stiffness. The open design results in excellent ventilation, particularly vital with dual wheels. Wheel hub and brake drum are of electric furnace iron, cast in one piece and machined on the same centers." The 7- x 2 9/16- x 7/32-inch frame featured four cross members. "With 25 years [actually 22 years] of *truck* engineering experience, Diamond T avoids excessive weight by use of special steel, by sturdy 'alligator-jaw' cross members, and by putting extra strength precisely where it belongs, instead of by mere rule-o'-thumb thickening of the whole frame structure, a practice often followed in cheaper construction." Shown above is the 1934 Model 211.
Detroit Public Library, National Automotive History Collection

"COMPLETE NEW LINE BY DIAMOND T MOTOR." *Automobile Topics*, December 8, 1934 featured the above photograph for its article covering the 1935 Diamond Ts. "For 1935 the Diamond T Motor Car Co. is offering a new complete line of 12 models from 1 1/2 to 5 tons capacity. The new model 220 [shown above] is…a 1 1/2-ton job…priced at $666." All of the 1935 models featured Diamond T's "exclusive 'Pressure Zone' Ventilation system." Twin scoops were located on the front of the hood sides and below the trim. Fresh air then passed through enclosed ducts to openings on both sides of the cab interior. This fresh air was "shielded from fumes and heat," important because "Fresh air keeps drivers wide awake—the surest accident protection." A Hercules-manufactured Diamond T Hurricane 6-cylinder 263-ci 85 HP engine powered the 12,000-pound GVW Model 220. The 1935 models offered customers the choice of the standard cab with a flat one-piece windshield and the DeLuxe three-man Vee-type cab. A Super-DeLuxe cab provided safety glass for all windows, fixed windshields, and "two-piece windows for controlled ventilation." The Model 220 shown is a DeLuxe model with chrome-plated equipment: the grille, "double beam head-lamps with foot control," an "ornamental radiator cap and hood fasteners," a "drop center spring bar bumper," and "giant hub caps." *Detroit Public Library, National Automotive History Collection*

Initially, identifying the 1933-1935 models can pose problems due to their similarity. All years featured the drop center spring bar bumper and similar grille designs. However, the 1933 models were equipped with rear hinged, front opening "suicide doors," dropped in 1934. The door handle and hinge locations are the distinguishing details. The 1933 and 1934 models featured "door-type hood louvers." The 1935 models replaced the louvers with decorative chrome grilles that featured a series of five horizontal strips and numerous vertical fins. The 1935 models featured a new lengthened hood design that extended to the cowl. The shorter hood on 1933 and 1934 models allowed a "door-type" vent to provide fresh air for the cab. For 1935, Diamond T provided the Pressure Zone Ventilation system that featured two hood scoops on each side of the lengthened hood to provide fresh air for the cab. Since the scoops were located at the front instead of the rear of the hood, the air was cleaner and cooler. While not identified, the truck shown above is probably a Model 351C or Model 352. Identical except for the engines supplied, a Hercules 6-cylinder 282-ci 76 HP engine powered the Model 351C while the Model 352 had a 303-ci 84 HP engine. *Detroit Public Library, National Automotive History Collection*

Above and opposite: Full color advertisements in the *Saturday Evening Post* featured beautifully illustrated paintings of the new 1936 models. Usually red with green trim, Diamond T's hallmark colors, the paintings illustrated an attention to style. By slightly exaggerating the truck's proportions, artists further emphasized the streamlined styling. Written copy often offered engineering details. These photographs accurately depict the attractive styling of the 1936 Diamond Ts without the artist's intentional distortions. Initially, the 1936 line of Diamond T trucks consisted of thirteen models. The 1 1/2- to 2 1/2-ton 11,000-pound Gross Vehicle Weight 212-A and 1 1/2- to 2-ton 11,500-pound 212-B, the 1 1/2- to 3-ton 12,000 pound Model 221, the 1 1/2- to 3-ton 12,000 pound Model 228, the 2- to 3- ton 13,000 pound Model 244, the 2- to 4-ton 15,000 pound Model 313, the 2- to 4-ton 15,000 pound Model 320, the 2 1/2- to 4-ton 16,000 pound Model 353, 2 1/2- to 4-ton 16,000 Model 360, 3- to 4-ton 17,500 pound Model 412-B, 4- to 5-ton 20,000 pound Model 412 DR (with double reduction axle), 4- to 5-ton 20,000 pound Model 512-B, and the 5- to 6 1/2-ton 24,000 pound Model 512-DR (with double reduction axle). Subsequently Diamond T introduced the 3/4-ton 8,000-pound Model 80. Added in late 1936 were two diesels. A 77-HP 260-ci Hercules DJXB powered the 1 1/2- to 3-ton 13,000 pound Model D20 and an 86-HP 298-ci Hercules DJXC powered the 2 1/2- to 4-ton 17,000 pound Model D30. *Detroit Public Library, National Automotive History Collection*

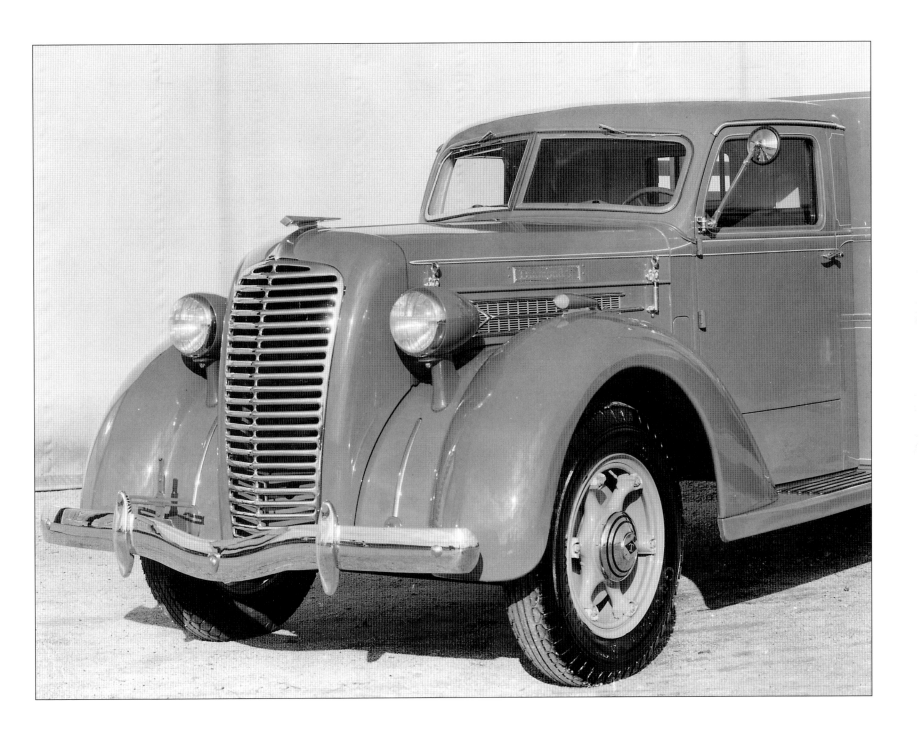

"The 1936 Diamond T will still be up-to-date when many another present-day truck has grown old and obsolete. Already, orders are pouring in from all parts of the world—at the highest rate in Diamond T history." The "up-to-date" 1936 1 1/2- to 3-ton Model 221 shown above was available with a standard 139 3/4-inch wheelbase and 151 3/4-, 163 3/4-, and 175 3/4-inch wheelbases were optional. The 263-ci 68 HP Diamond T "Hurricane Six' engine manufactured by Hercules was moved forward in the chassis for better balance, increased cab and body room." Diamond T sales brochures and advertisements emphasized the mounting design and quality of its engines. The engine was "cushion floated and cradled in a four-point rubber mounting of exclusive Diamond T design. These mountings permit no metal-to-metal contact…the great Diamond T engine supplies a flow of power that is almost as smooth as steam." The "seven-bearing crankshaft of chrome molybdenum steel carries six integral counterweights…which reduces the stresses and unit loads on the main bearings, for longer life in hard service." The frame on the Model 221 was "individually designed for each wheelbase, with heavy 1/4" stock and six cross members." Channel sections measured 8 1/16" x 3 1/32" x 1/4". *Lon Arbegust Collection*

"Smart New Streamlines! Brilliant New Engineering!" Diamond T introduced the 1936 models with emphasis on both style and substance. *Automobile Topics*, December 9, 1935, featured the above photograph of the 1 1/2- to 2-ton Model 212-A tractor and reflected the themes of style and engineering in its article on the new models. "In announcing the new line of 1936 models which range from 1 1/2 to 4 tons capacity, Diamond T Motor Car Company stresses a further development of its well known streamline style as well as important advances in load distribution, spring suspension, vibration elimination, driver comfort and increased ease of handling." However, the article concluded, "In spite of the importance [of] mechanical construction, first place goes to new appearance…. In this connection it is worth noting that all Diamond T designs are personally originated and carried to completion by Mr. C.A. Tilt, President of the Diamond T Motor Car Company." With that in mind take note of the 30-degree slope of the Vee-type windshield, compared to the 11-degree slope of the 1935 models, as well as the redesigned radiator grille. The 212 (A-B) Series replaced the 211 (A-B) Series, increasing payload from 10,000 to 11,500 pounds while retaining the same 63-HP 228-ci Hercules engine. *Detroit Public Library, National Automotive History Collection*

"The new 1936 Diamond T is just this: a very fine truck made still finer. *Refined* mechanically—yet without a single major change in any unit, because millions of hard working miles for thousands of owners have shown the fitness of these famous Diamond T features. Engines, axles, brakes, clutches, transmissions, springs—time proved and unaltered. Style advanced beyond anything in the industry." Diamond T specifications noted numerous mechanical refinements. The 30-gallon gasoline tank was die formed and welded not soldered. Armored wiring provided "the most workmanlike, permanent, short-proof, break-proof job of wiring to be found among motor trucks...no dangling, chafing loops and tangles." As a result the engine compartment was "exceptionally clean." The new frame on the 1936 models featured deeper sections and six cross members for "greater strength and stiffness." Diamond T clutch and brake pedals "pivoted on a solid mounting, attached to the left frame member. They are thus completely isolated from all engine and running gear shocks." The result: "Twelve cylinder smoothness" in a 6-cylinder truck. "The Diamond T engine simply does not overheat." The water pump "circulates more than 50 gallons of water per minute at open throttle." *Lon Arbegust Collection*

"There has never been a cab like this. When a man takes the wheel of the new Diamond T, he gets a new respect for his truck, his employer, for his job—and for himself." Respect would also come from the cab's construction for one driver. Diamond T would tell his story to make the point that the new De Luxe cab, while stylish, was also well constructed and safe. "On a dark night," driver Glen Woodward misjudged the height of a 30-ton pedestrian bridge running into it with his semi-trailer. The bridge was "dragged from its emplacement, fell four feet, sharp edge down, directly onto the roof of the cab where he was sitting. The terrific impact of the bridge dented the roof—but that was all. Driver Woodward [and his 'helper'] climbed safely out, for both steel doors would still open and shut... Diamond T's all-steel roof construction had saved a life...." The Diamond T tractor in the photograph above is similar to Woodward's Diamond T. While not identified, the tractor may be a 1 1/2- to 3-ton 12,000 pound Gross vehicle Weight Model 221 or a 2- to 4-ton 15,000 pound Model 320. A 6-cylinder 68 HP 263-ci engine powered the Model 221, with a 76-HP 282-ci engine in the Model 320. Tractors featured a 139 3/4-inch wheelbase. *Detroit Public Library, National Automotive History Collection*

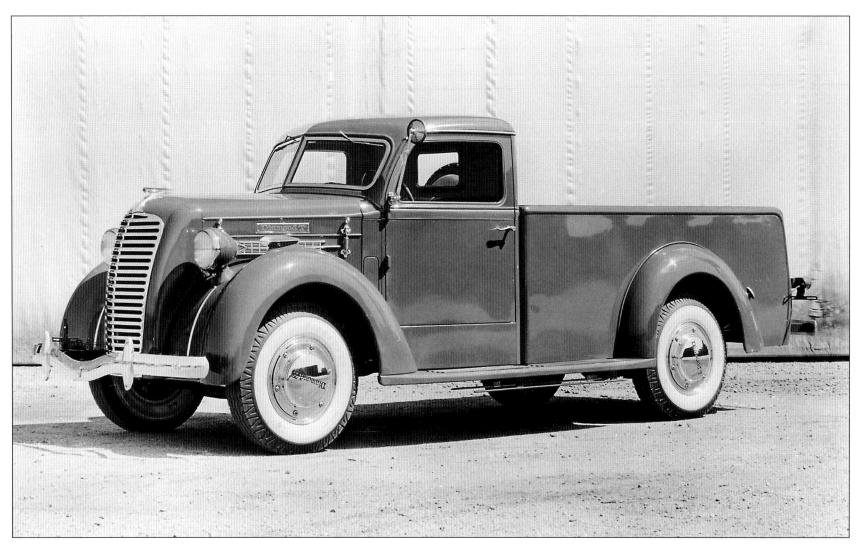

Above and opposite: "An entirely new Diamond T delivery truck of three-quarter ton capacity has been announced…. This newest Diamond T, while similar in general appearance to the larger Diamond T trucks, represents fresh engineering and designing throughout the chassis, cab and bodies. The manufacturer's announced purpose in developing this truck has been to provide for the requirements of truck operators in the field between the familiar 1/2-ton light delivery type of commercial car chassis and the 1 1/2-ton heavy duty truck." *Automobile Topics,* June 22, 1936 featured this copy and the photograph of Diamond T's new Model 80 shown above. A 190-ci Hercules six-cylinder engine featuring seven main bearings powered the 119-inch wheelbase Model 80. Diamond T conducted a series of mileage tests and announced that on "comparatively long runs, with infrequent stops in normal suburban and country highway traffic, 20 and 21 miles per gal. were consistently recorded." Diamond T emphasized the "new type of X-frame especially developed to provide a solid foundation of extreme rigidity." It featured "6-inch side rails" with "eight-inch X-type bracing." White sidewall tires, chrome wheel covers, and the "streamline radiator shell" gave this Model 80 with an 8-foot "express body" the "distinctive Diamond T appearance…that sets you apart from the crowd." Added later was a "pick-up" body option. *Detroit Public Library, National Automotive History Collection*

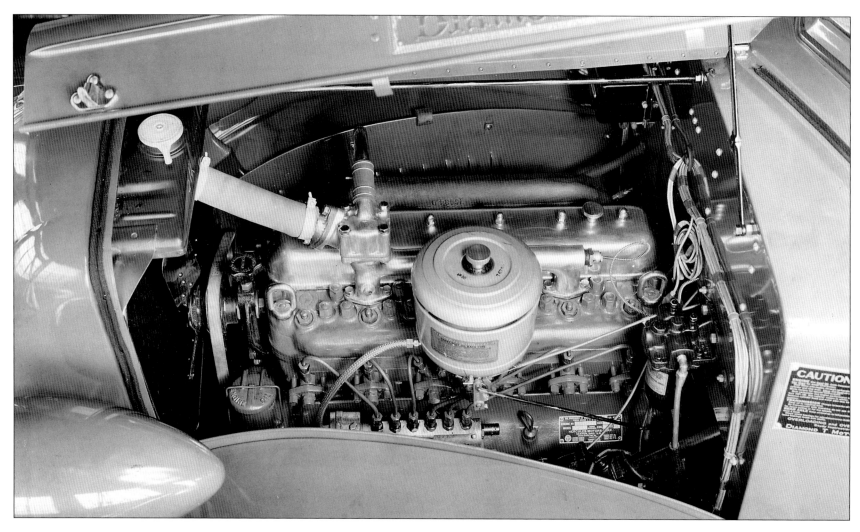

"The one truck engine deliberately designed to battle abuse with every safeguard that science affords." Hercules Motors Corporation, Canton, Ohio built the Diamond T Super Service engine, shown inside the compartment of a 1936 model, to Diamond T specifications. Hercules also supplied engines to numerous truck manufacturers including Autocar, Federal, Kenworth, Mack, and Reo. Diamond T sales material stressed the difference between an engine designed for the demands of truck service and passenger car service. Some manufacturers used passenger car engines "only because it costs the manufacturer considerably less." A truck engine hauls significantly larger loads and as a result makes far more revolutions per mile because of the greater gear reduction needed to provide the power to handle these loads. Trucks, Diamond T pointed out; also cover many more miles per year than passenger cars. Features Diamond T highlighted included an "engine block of electric furnace chrome-molybdenum-nickel iron" that was "about 25% harder" and more resistant to warping and wear than ordinary iron. Zollner light alloy pistons allowed faster acceleration and produced less vibration and load on the bearings. Cadmium-nickel bearings replaced babbitt bearings that softened at "very moderate engine temperatures." The engines also featured seven main bearings, a counter-balanced crankshaft, "tocco" electric hardened crankshaft journals, and a "full-pressure lubricating system with a Duo-Flo oil filter." *Detroit Public Library, National Automotive History Collection*

"Model 80…Diamond T's sensational response to new-day delivery needs!" Shown with the standard 8-foot panel body, this 3/4-ton Model 80 clearly displays "Its smart, fresh STREAMLINED STYLE…consistent with Diamond T, the world-originator of style in motor trucks." Modern appearance could also be functional. The new 1936 De Luxe Vee-type safety steel cab "makes driving a pleasure…. It's as comfortable as a pleasure car, as attractive as a pleasure car, and a whole lot more practical than the driving compartments of most of them!" This 60-inch wide cab "finished in costly oven-baked enamel" featured doors with cushioned armrests, compartments above the windshield and in the door "for order-book, maps, smokes or similar articles." The "streamline Vee-type twin windshields [were] individually controlled by separate cranks" and featured "two automatic windshield wipers." The De Luxe cab also featured a green and buff dash panel. The adjustable seat cushion and back were "comfortably upholstered in an attractive green." The $525 "standard chassis at the factory" Model 80 was equipped with Lockheed hydraulic brakes with 14-inch diameter 2-inch wide drums, a 10-inch diameter single plate clutch, a three-speed transmission "with synchro-mesh second speed and silent helical gears, and a full floating spiral bevel rear axle." *Detroit Public Library, National Automotive History Collection*

"The truck of the year is here! A great new addition to a great truck line. There is no other truck quite like this new Diamond T. It fills a gap which has long existed between the light delivery vehicle and the heavy-duty 1 1/2-ton, which is too often too large and too heavy for best economy." In 1937, Diamond T introduced the Model 301 with styling similar to the Model 80. The $595 1 1/2-ton 10,000-pound GVW model, designed to accommodate a 10-foot body on the standard 135-inch wheelbase, featured a new 66 HP 6-cylinder 221-ci Hercules engine. The engine featured full pressure lubrication and full-length water jackets to cool the cylinders. According to *Automobile Topics*, July 5, 1937, "engine mounting is the special four point 'cushion cradle' rubber suspension with torque arm developed by Diamond T to isolate engine vibration from the frame. A special linkage allows clutch and brake pedals and master cylinder to be rigidly attached to the frame and unaffected by movement of the engine and power line." Like the Model 80, the Model 301 featured 16-inch wheels and available white sidewall tires and full chrome "hub-caps." Larger 20-inch wheels were an option. *Automobile Topics* and the *Commercial Car Journal* featured the above photograph. *Detroit Public Library, National Automotive History Collection*

"The new Streamliners of the Highways. Diamond T Cab-Over-Engine Trucks. The newest, freshest style note in the motor truck industry! There isn't a single 'borrowed' line in the Cab-Over-Engine design. Perfect visibility—impressive, smart appearance—extremely practical, with none of the top-heavy look so often seen. Wide Vee windshield—flush radiator grille, strong and handsome—well placed headlights." *Commercial Car Journal*, November 1937 featured the above photograph and noted, "The appearance of these [1938] models presents a radical departure from the conventional. It is not like any other cab-over-engine truck, and is equally different from the Diamond T standard line." Hercules engines, designated as Diamond T Super Service engines, powered each of the five models initially offered. The 68 HP 228-ci JXA for Models 401 and 402, the 78 HP 263-ci JXB for Model 507, the 84-HP 282-ci JXC for Model 607, and the 84-HP 320-ci JXD for Model 609. All of the Cab-Over-Engine models were available with "straight frames" with wheelbases of 96, 108, 120, and 132 inches to accommodate bodies from 10 to 16 feet in length. Tractors were available only with a 96-inch wheelbase. 168-, 180-, and 192-inch wheelbase options were available with "double drop frames" for 20- to 24-foot length bodies, especially buses. *Detroit Public Library, National Automotive History Collection*

The Diamond T compared the Cab-Over-Engine models to railroad streamliners in advertisements that also featured the Burlington Zephyr. "Like a modern railway locomotive, it restyles the industry. Wherever it goes, this strikingly handsome vehicle tells the world its owner is thoroughly modern-minded, progressive." No longer new, this "Streamliner of the Highways," Diamond T Cab-Over-Engine tractor, photographed in 1948, features the optional sleeper cab. By 1941, Diamond T stylists had changed the styling of the "streamline locomotive type cowl and radiator grille." A single 13-chrome rib version replaced the louvers bisected by a horizontal molding strip that started at the back door of the cab. (See the photograph on the previous page.) This particular truck still has this strip, but only on the door. More powerful Hercules engines powered six models, ranging from the 1 1/2-ton Model 404C to the 5-7 ton Model 806C. "For major engine overhaul, the unique, practical and enormously rigid Diamond T sub-Frame Assembly permits the entire power unit, including transmission and radiator," to be rolled out for servicing. The insulated engine housing "when removed gave access to the downdraft carburetor, oil bath air cleaner, fuel lines, coil, distributor and engine wiring." Removable fender shields provided access to the rest of the engine. The 75-inch wide De Luxe cab featured "Thick, highly efficient insulation employed throughout, including engine housing, floor, doors and roof [that] means all-weather comfort." *Lon Arbegust Collection*

The 1938 "Fast Dispatch" Model 201 features the all steel pick-up body. The steel spoke wheels shown were standard, but usually covered by the chrome full wheel covers Diamond T featured to emphasize its styling leadership. The De Luxe "engine-turned instrument panel" that featured an electric clock and cigar lighter was available on the three Fast Dispatch models. A stylish "banjo-type steering wheel" with a "ring-type horn control" was also part of the De Luxe cab. The 10,000-pound gross vehicle weight 1- to 1 1/2-ton "Fast Dispatch" Model 305 was available with either a standard 135-inch or optional 150-inch wheelbase. A 221-ci 66 HP Hercules QXC3 engine supplied the power. The Model 306 was a "straight 1 1/2-ton model with a gross rating of 11,000 lbs." This 150-inch wheelbase model featured the same engine as the Model 305. While the Model 201 had a 3-speed transmission, the Model 305 and Model 306 had 4-speed versions. *Power Wagon* and *Commercial Car Journal* noted that the Model 306 was equipped with the newly introduced 17-inch truck tire, with "capacity practically equal to the 20-inch size." Each "Fast Dispatch" model was available with up to 20-inch tires as well as dual rear tires. *Lon Arbegust Collection*

"Economy can wear a top hat! You don't save anything by operating an old truck nor by buying a homely one. The old truck costs more to run and the homely one costs just as much to buy as a Diamond T." This advertising appeal to both substance and style reflected a continuing Diamond T theme. *Commercial Car Journal,* October 1939 featured Diamond T's new Cab-Forward models. They complemented the full Cab-Over-Engine models were first introduced in 1937. According to Diamond T sales literature "The Diamond T Cab-Forward models present an outstanding engineering achievement in the saving of almost three feet of wheelbase with no appreciable loss or disadvantage of any kind. Height is only slightly greater—only two low steps to the cab floor, as usual. Comfort and ease of handling are at least equal. The 60" steel cab is fitted with two large form-fitting individual seats, deep-cushioned, and angled for the most restful driving position." Diamond T offered the 1 1/2- to 2-ton Model 306SC and the 1 1/2- to 3-ton Model 404SC. A 6-cylinder 69 HP 221-ci Hercules CBQXC3 engine powered the Model 306SC shown above. The Model 404SC featured the "larger and more powerful" 6-cylinder 76 HP 245-ci Hercules CBJXE3 engine. *Lon Arbegust Collection*

The Model 306SC, shown above, carried a gross vehicle weight rating of 11,000 pounds and a base chassis price of $775. The 13,000-pound GVW Model 404SC had a base chassis price of $885. Both models featured a "full-floating spiral bevel, extra heavy" rear axle. A "dual range heavy-duty, full-floating two-speed rear axle" was available as an extra cost option "only with 20" wheels—17" tires could not be used. The 7 1/2- x 3- x 1/4-inch "pressed steel frame on the Model 306SC featured tapering side rails and six cross members, "individually designed for each wheelbase." The front cross member was "extra wide and deep, for positive protection from 'weaving' at this point." The engine was "cushion-cradled in a four-point rubber mounting of new design which absorbs vibration almost completely." The "latest type" Lockheed hydraulic brakes had a lining area of 253 square inches for all four wheels. A B-K Vacuum booster was optional. Both Cab-Forward models were equipped with "Double-acting" hydraulic shock absorbers on the "front end." The semi-elliptical "silico-man-

ganese steel springs shackled with Diamond T compression type rubber bushings" never required lubrication. Both models featured four speed transmissions. Ross "cam and lever steering with a roller bearing cam-follower" was standard. The steering column was adjustable for angle. *Lon Arbegust Collection*

The Pak-Age-Car manufactured by the Package Car Corporation, Chicago, and introduced in 1927, initially sold through the sales organization of the Stutz Motor Car Company. Writing in the January 1928 issue of the *Journal of the Society of Automotive Engineers*, Lee Oldfield, "consulting engineer in charge of design and development" of the vehicle, noted, "One field of highway transportation service that the motor vehicle has not heretofore successfully invaded is house-to-house delivery, especially of milk. The short distance between stops, the relatively long waits between vehicle movements, and the intelligence of the horse…give the single horse-and-wagon unit a low operating cost…." According to Oldfield, stable facilities were becoming increasingly difficult to find thus "forcing operators to adopt motorized equipment." The "vehicle was designed for the specific purpose of replacing the single horse-drawn vehicle," according to Oldfield. The result was the unique frameless Pak-Age-Car. Initially developed as a concept in 1913, the "incomparably more sanitary than animal-drawn" 1800-pound vehicle had a load capacity of 3000 pounds. There was no front axle. A pair of transverse suspension springs connected the wheels to the body "made entirely of steel and metal-veneer panels." This early version featured a center mounted steering wheel. *MoToR* magazine's July 1927 coverage of the Pak-Age-Car featured the above photograph. *Detroit Public Library, National Automotive History Collection*

A 1935 sales brochure for the 1936 "New Stutz Pak-Age Car" declared, "The Pak-Age-Car is not a compromise with conventional construction. It is not a truck, but a tool designed specifically for the use of industries engaged in frequent-stop house-to-house delivery of merchandise." *Automobile Topics*, November 11, 1935 featured the new vehicle. This newer version of the original model introduced in 1927 continued to feature a removable power unit. Referred to as the "Mechanical Horse," the 4-cylinder 113-inch 1XA Hercules engine and "all its accessories, the clutch, the transmission and final drive [were] all assembled as a unit in conjunction with the rear springs, hubs, wheels, service brakes and tires." As shown, the Mechanical Horse was easily removable for servicing without disturbing the load. A complete replacement could be installed in the shop or in an emergency the exchange could "even be made on the street with a minimum loss of time." The new version featured a 90-inch wheelbase compared to the original 92 1/2-inch length. Overall length was now 158 inches, up from the original 123 1/2-inch length. Width increased from 53 to 65 1/4 inches. The steering wheel was now on the left side of the interior. A storage area replaced the center-mounted steering wheel. *Detroit Public Library, National Automotive History Collection*

"From Now On! The famous Pak-Age-Car, pioneer of door-to-door delivery economy, becomes the Diamond T Pak-Age-Car, mechanically better than ever and backed by the industry's strongest independent truck builder!" According to the *Commercial Car Journal*, April 1939, effective March 10, 1939, Diamond T took over the sales and service of Pak-Age-Car. Prior to this change the Pak-Age-Car Corporation located in Connersville, Indiana had introduced two models for 1939. The Model 117, a 184-inch long 116-inch wheelbase version, was available along with the 90-inch wheelbase 158-inch long Model 91 (Shown above.). Now referred to as the "Iron Horse," a 32 horsepower 4-cylinder Lycoming engine supplied power for both models. While adding its distinctive emblem to the front of the vehicle, Diamond T continued to offer the Pak-Age-Car virtually unchanged. Even the model numbers were continued. Production of the Diamond T models also continued at the Connersville plant. The April 20, 1940 *Diamond T Sales Bulletin* was devoted entirely to the Diamond T Pak-Age-Car. "Twelve months of real progress, of increasing recognition and acceptance, of further development and refinement—that's the story of the first year of the Diamond T Pak-Age-Car." The Diamond T Pak-Age-Car featured Bendix hydraulic brakes on all four wheels with 200 square inches of lining area. *Detroit Public Library, National Automotive History Collection*

"Heavy-duty hauling on the *Highway to Victory*.... Diamond T Trucks. Along the road to Germany and Japan—the Highway to Victory—there's a long, tough haul still to be made. And as the Stars and Stripes push forward, American fighting men are learning what American truck owners have known for years—that Diamond T trucks have the built-in ruggedness and stamina to stand up under extreme conditions. On every fighting front, Diamond T army vehicles are proving their heritage from the Diamond T trucks at home—trucks that are rolling up hundreds of thousands of miles under the heaviest transport burden in history." Like other manufacturers, Diamond T continued to advertise during World War II. In part the ads were a reminder of the key role Diamond T trucks were playing on the battlefront. It was also an opportunity to remind the readers that Diamond T trucks were also crucial to the home front battles to provide the essential supplies needed to meet the nation's war production needs. Shown above is the personnel carrier version of the 4-ton "Six-by-Six" Army "Prime mover," designed and manufactured exclusively by Diamond T. These trucks, also modified as wreckers and pontoon carriers, were equipped with a front-end power winch. *Lon Arbegust Collection*

"Diamond T 'tank-movers' speed desert warfare. This grim Diamond T in 'war paint' is *your* truck. It's in the fight for Liberty, for you and all of us. Enormous Diamond T diesel six-wheelers such as this, with gross truck and trailers capacity of nearly a hundred tons, move massive army tanks at high speeds—forward to combat zones and back for repairs. When Victory is won, men who are now battling in far places can tell you many a tale of how well these and other types of Diamond T Trucks served them." Such ads, featuring the "tank-mover" shown, helped keep the Diamond T name before the post-war consumer. They also reminded the Diamond T owner of his wartime obligations. "Meanwhile, all your patience and ingenuity and care are called upon. The new trucks that you may need are not to be had. Your veteran Diamond T Trucks have got to last—to stay on the job—to clothe and feed and safeguard civilian life and health. That means they've got to be cared for skillfully and systematically. The Diamond T Life Extension Lubrication and Inspection Service—backed and sealed by the solemn Victory Pledge of Driver, Dealer, and Owner, is ready to cover every Diamond T…. It's for the duration." *Lon Arbegust Collection*

"If you want to know, ask Texaco about Diamond T reliability. The great Texaco fleet of Diamond T's has been more than twenty years in the building. The Texas Company's experience with Diamond T dates back to the four-cylinder days of solid tires and two-wheel brakes. With many hundreds of Diamond T trucks in service with continuing reorders over more than two decades, The Texas Company and its distributors provide convincing and continuing evidence of their confidence in 'Diamond T reliability.'" The "Extra-Heavy-Duty" models, introduced in 1940, featured a flat grille while the "Heavy-Duty" models continued to feature a rounded grille. The turn signal marker light on the fender generally appeared on post-war models. As a result, the Extra-Heavy-Duty Texaco-owned "six-wheeler" shown was part of a lineup that featured the non-diesel-powered Model 806, 809, and 901. The tractor shown above is probably a Model 901. A 7-bearing 572-ci 6-cylinder 190 HP Continental R6572 engine supplied power. These engines featured a "one-piece cylinder block cast of special fine-grain alloy iron." The five ring aluminum alloy pistons included "two oil rings for accurate control of cylinder lubrication." Diamond T specified that the "maximum train rating" for these six-wheel tractors was 76,000 pounds. *Lon Arbegust Collection*

"Your trucks are your ambassadors. They're often the only thing by which the public can judge you. That's why Diamond T builds smart trucks and nothing else. Diamond T style is good business—for everybody." Dairy Despatch Co., Dubuque, Iowa may have had this theme in mind when it chose the "DeLuxe" version of the Diamond T Cab-Forward Models as its "ambassador." Optional equipment available only on the DeLuxe versions included the "chrome-plated giant hubcaps" on the Model 509SC tractor shown above. Diamond T touted the "Vee-type steel cab, of unequaled distinction of appearance." The "exceptionally roomy and comfortable" 60-inch wide cab featured a "one-piece steel roof, sound and heat insulated" with "Streamline Vee-type twin windshields, individually controlled by separate cranks." The cab also featured "two automatic windshield wipers, chrome finished hardware and rear-view mirror, windshield frames of stainless steel, domelight, adjustable sun visor, glove compartment, cushioned armrests, [and a] rubber floor mat." The seats had "durable and comfortable air spring cushions…more than seven inches in depth, finished in Diamond T tan." Customers could also have chosen the optional "banjo-type jar-absorbing safety steering wheel" to complement the "light buff" interior and the cab's standard "DeLuxe engine-turned instrument panel with electric cigar-lighter and electrically operated clock." *Lon Arbegust Collection*

EXCHANGE LUMBER & MFG. CO.

EXCHANGE LUMBER&MFG.CO.
GLENWOOD PRODUCTS
GLEN. 1621

Diamond T

While Diamond T heavily promoted style as a strong feature of its trucks, this muddy Model 509SC Tractor, shown in a 1947 photograph, demonstrates that clean or dirty, the ultimate proof of a truck's worth is its ability to get the assigned job done. The 2- to 3 1/2-ton 106-inch wheelbase Specification 1 Model 509SC, designed to accommodate tractor-trailer service, had an 8 1/16- x 3 1/32- x 1/4-inch pressed steel, tapering side-rail frame. Six cross members, including three alligator-jaw type members provided "exceptional strength and stiffness." A 6-cylinder 282-ci 99 HP Hercules CBJXC engine powered the model. According to Diamond T sales literature "The floor is exceptionally 'clean' and the driver enters or leaves through either door with ease. Gearshift control is conveniently placed, with the shifting tower between the seats, where it causes no interference." The "engine cover is low and heavily insulated with rock-wool, as is also the toe-board, so that the engine heat is fully excluded. The engine cover is held in place by three spring fasteners—instantly removable." In addition, there were two removable inspection plates on each side of the "hood" area. The absence of chrome and painted trim on this model compared to the initial Cab Forward models indicates its production shortly before the end of production in early 1942. An "H" designated models equipped with heavy-duty oversize rear axles. *Lon Arbegust Collection*

It's 1948, and the truck shown here and on the next page are Diamond T's "tank-mover" produced for the military in World War II [see page 70]. The "Enormous Diamond T diesel six-wheelers, with gross truck and trailer capacity of nearly a *hundred tons* [that] move massive army tanks at high speeds—forward to combat zones or back for repairs," were featured in Diamond T wartime advertisements. The hood louvers are identical to the military vehicles as is the vent on the cab roof—neither featured on Diamond T civilian trucks produced before or after the war. The compartment on the running board behind the cab and the metal panels below the cab door are also identical to the "tank-movers." Unlike the truck shown, the post-war Model 910s featured slightly curved front fenders. The military trucks had these flat fenders. The post-war models also featured headlights located closer to the hood. The more massive bumper including the opening on the left side was also a feature of the military "tank-mover." Red Top Trucking has subsequently modified the truck for service as a fifth wheel-equipped tractor. The military vehicle had trailers to haul tanks attached like a wagon to a farm tractor. *Lon Arbegust Collection*

The Diamond T Deluxe Sleeper cab featured on this Model 910 featured a frame of "heavy hardwood understructure reinforced with angle irons." The cab panels consisted of "Auto-body sheet metal [with] full rounded corners and skirting to frame level at rear of cab." The roof featured "French type metal roof corners with water-proof decking in [the] center over padding and plywood, felt insulated on underside. Drip mouldings above doors and windows." The sleeper cab windows were stationary. "High grade textile leather [was] used for all cushions and mattress. Interior sides [were] lined with textile leather to match cushions." The cab's sleeper portion provided a "large compartment under the bunk for luggage or extra fuel tank, with flush doors on each side controlled by [an] inside latch." The 1000-pound cab measured 94 3/4 inches from the front axle to the back of the cab and 81 inches in overall width at the rear of the cab. The sleeping compartment measured 72 x 23 inches. A Timken 36021 TW front axle was standard on all Model 910s. Diamond T offered the standard single-speed full-floating dual reduction Timken U-200-P and the double reduction two speed Timken U-300-P with "two sets of helical gears in final drive" rear axles. *Leroy Gurganus Collection*

"Towering above the field in speed, power, economy…That's Diamond T *reliability*. Today's Diamond T trucks are the finest we have ever built. They haul maximum loads at minimum costs in every kind of service with the built-in Diamond T reliability famous since 1905." The emphasis on "*reliability*" was a prominent theme following World War II. It was likely to have been a factor in Merchants Freight Service's decision to purchase the Model 910 shown above. A 6-cylinder 672-ci 150 HP Cummins diesel powered the Model 910. In comparison, the similar in size and capacity non-diesel Model 901 featured a 6-cylinder 572-ci 190 HP Continental R6572 gasoline engine. Buyers of Model 910 "six-wheelers" had the option of four Timken dual drive tandem rear axles. The worm drive SW3010PA was limited to "high-speed highway service," while the worm drive SW3012PA was not. The "heavier and more rugged with greater load capacity" SW456P also featured worm drive. The SD462P employed double reduction drive, with the first reduction through a spiral bevel gear and the second reduction through helical spur gears. GVW capacity for these dual axle models was 40,000 and 50,000 pounds. Tandem axle model wheelbase options included 188 3/4, 206 3/4, 224 3/4, and 236 3/4 inches. *Leroy Gurganus Collection*

"America's Best Looking and Best *Built* Truck. From their low, streamlined, functional beauty to their bright stainless steel grilles and trim, Diamond T trucks are quite generally acknowledged to be the handsomest on the road. This traditional fine appearance, however, is not just superficial 'frosting.' Experienced truck men recognize it as the outward expression of long-lived internal excellence that has earned Diamond T a position of unquestioned leadership in reducing hauling costs on all kinds of jobs." According to Diamond T advertising, part of the "functional beauty" was "the cab the driver leaves with regret. From the shining flat sheets of fine steel, straight through to the beautifully finished, upholstered unit, ready to begin its years of comfort service on a Diamond T chassis, the famous Diamond T DeLuxe Cab is McLaughlin-built. You'll find it enduringly quiet, excellently insulated, comfortably cushioned, handsomely fitted and trimmed." The McLaughlin Body Company, Moline, Illinois, used "giant presses [to] smoothly contour a single piece of steel into Diamond T's handsome streamlined style." The truck shown above was part of the 23,000 to 28,000-pound GVW "extra-heavy duty" 1949 Model 702A, 806A, and 806AH series that featured the 6-cylinder 404-ci 138 HP Hercules WXLD engine. "Full air Westinghouse type" brakes were standard. *Lon Arbegust Collection*

"Announcing the New 1950 Super-Service Diamond T's. Three new Super Value Models blanket the 1 1/2- to 5-ton field with Efficiency, Accessibility, Comfort and Safety *beyond all previous standards!*" Diamond T returned to a long-standing theme when it referred to these new models as "America's handsomest motor trucks." Sales literature noted, "Your customers may never see your offices or plant. But they *do* see your *trucks* and are influenced by their appearance. That's why Diamond T has always devoted extra effort to making its trucks the *best-looking* on the road." The December 1949 *Commercial Car Journal* covered the new Diamond T Model 420, 520, and 620. The article noted "Accessibility is the keynote of the new design, with the development of a 'quick detachable' front fender assembly providing easy access to all work below the cylinder head." A mechanic could accomplish the removal of each fender in three minutes. The small vents visible on the hood supplied fresh air to the under-the-hood engine air cleaner. Hercules-manufactured gasoline engines supplied power for the new models. The front axles were moved back 9 3/4 inches closer to the rear of the cab for "easier handling, shorter turns and a better ride for both driver and load." *Leroy Gurganus Collection*

"The sensational new Diamond T cab is almost *ten inches wider*. Heavy gauge steel is die-formed and welded for greatest possible strength and safety. Greater visibility! Windshield has no center post—it's one single piece of curved laminated safety plate glass." Diamond T sales material noted the new 69-inch wide "full-vision safety steel cab," manufactured by International Harvester, was the "same size and construction as [the] cab on Diamond T's big diesels costing as much as $15,000!" The cab featured two parallel mounted electric windshield wipers and a removable stainless steel panel for instruments and controls. Diamond T added models to its initial offering of three models. In its April 1950 issue, *Commercial Car Journal* reported, "Diamond T has added a new low-priced 1 1/2-ton Model 322 in the volume production field, rated for 14,500 lb gross vehicle weight." A 6-cylinder 7-bearing 236-ci 91 HP Diamond T-Hercules QXLD "Super-Service Engine" powered the new model that featured a standard 130-inch wheelbase. A "Rugged Oversize Tube and Fin Radiator" with a 587 square inch frontal area was a "best in class" feature. As the "moving billboard" indicates, Diamond T continued the 100,000-mile or one-year factory warranty, introduced in November 1939, on the new "Super-Service" models. *Lon Arbegust Collection*

"New 1950 Diamond T's set completely new standards of motor truck design. You're looking at the ultra-modern version of 'the truck of lowest cost'—the handsome new 1950 Diamond T that embodies everything you've always said a fine truck should have!" May 6, 1950 *Saturday Evening Post* advertising announced, "New low prices begin at $1690 for [the] 1 1/2-ton Model 322. Standard chassis and cab at factory (taxes extra)." Advertisements for the new models often featured trucks in Diamond T Red with green accents. A green stainless steel band with "Diamond-T" is clearly visible on the cab door and would become a long-standing Diamond T feature. According to the *Commercial Car Journal*, April 1950, the cab featured "A new mounting system [that] floats cab and sheet metal as a single rigid unit entirely isolated from the effects of frame distortion. Cab, cowl, fenders, hood and radiator support are locked together into a truss-type structure that maintains accurate alignment with no relative movement between any of the parts. This unit is carried by a rubber and spring-mounted rocker-arm at the rear of the cab and a similar flexible mounting under the radiator support channel, with a lighter intermediate mounting at each side of the frame." *Lon Arbegust Collection*

Diamond T advertised the new 1950 "ultra-modern" Model 322, 420, 520, and 620, explaining these models "are in production now." The ad further noted, "A companion 1-ton Model 222 will also be available in the near future." Shown above is the Model 222 with a pick-up body. This truck was part of a long tradition of pick-up and delivery trucks offered by Diamond T that dates to the 1923 Special Delivery Model 75 "designed for high speed light delivery work." This was Diamond T's response to the Reo Speed Wagon, introduced in 1915. *Commercial Car Journal* referred to this class of trucks as "Speed Trucks." By 1926, Diamond T offered a one-ton capacity Model 76. In 1936, the 3/4-ton Model 80 with an 8-foot "express body" and "pick-up" body option was offered. The "Fast Dispatch" Model 201, introduced in mid-1938, was one of three "Fast Dispatch" models offered for the 1- to 1 1/2-ton field. A "De Luxe Open Express" body and an all steel "Pick-Up Express" body were available. Each "Fast Dispatch" model was available with up to 20-inch tires as well as dual rear tires. The 1950 Model 222 featured the "sensational new Diamond T No-Draft, Full-Vision, Safety Steel Cab supplied with all the new models." *Leroy Gurganus Collection*

"This Diamond T is built as fine as it looks! Whatever the size of your company, [the] handsome Diamond T is an impressive 'advertisement on wheels' that will make new friends for you. But this external beauty is only a reflection of the internal excellence which Diamond T engineers have built into every detail. Excellence that has made Diamond T the acknowledged leader in reducing costs on all sorts of jobs." Diamond T was a Cummins Diesel customer and Cummins returned the favor for a truck used at its St. Paul, Minnesota, sales and service branch. Diamond T referred to the new International Harvester-manufactured cab as the "World's Finest Cab." A noted feature was the "large removable cover in [the] cab floor [that] permits inspection and service of [the] transmission. The front cab cross-member is built in three pieces with [a] removable center section to facilitate disassembly or removal of transmission. Special provision has been made for easy inspection and filling of [the] master cylinder, with a separate cover plate in the floor on the left side of cab directly over [the] master cylinder." Throughout the 1950s, Diamond T continued to upgrade and add models to its medium-duty line. *Lon Arbegust Collection*

"A higher standard of highway performance…New Diamond T Model 622, 141 horsepower—40,000 lbs. gross train weight. This newest Diamond T is built for the highway hauler who wants top performance at bottom cost—with tractor-trailer gross weights to 40,000 lbs. Cost is important, too. First cost and operating cost. Model 622 is not the largest Diamond T. It is specifically designed to haul 35,000 to 40,000 gross faster, smoother, and at lower cost than anything that has ever been built before." This advertising copy from the April 1952 *Commercial Car Journal* was followed in the June issue with a news story. The article noted, "For 'HIGH OUTPUT' performance in the 2 1/2- to 5-ton field, a new Model 622 Diamond T has been developed around the [330-ci] 141 hp overhead-valve Continental K6330 engine." A nearly identical April 1953 advertisement continued to refer to the "New" Model 622 "now available with the new 363 cubic-inch overhead valve engine—150 truck horsepower." The Model 622 sales brochure described this engine's "sodium filled exhaust valves," explaining "The fluid sodium drains heat rapidly from head to stem where bronze guides carry it off to the cooling water. Large intake valves are of heat-resistant silchrome alloy steel. Dual valve springs are cadmium plated for longer life." *Lon Arbegust Collection*

"At Diamond T we believe that every truck must be built to the highest standards of quality and performance that we know—and should look the part. That is why the fine alloy steels and precision workmanship of every Diamond T are matched by similar care in design, appearance and finish." Among the quality components Diamond T sales material highlighted on the Model 622 was the 8 1/16- x 3 3/32- x 1/4-inch frame. "Frame design is commonly a compromise between the opposing demands for ample strength and the minimum weight. Diamond T achieves both as the result of a highly developed design with full depth of siderails from rear of front springs to front of rear springs. Exceptional stiffness is achieved by use of six cross members, including two of alligator-jaw design." Model 622 tractors, such as the example shown above, were available in 130- or 142-inch wheelbase lengths. "Heavy-Duty transmissions…were an outstanding and exclusive feature. Both standard and overdrive transmissions have forward control so that the cab floor is clear. Gears and shafts are of heat-treated electric furnace alloy steel of large diameter and carried on ball and roller bearings." Optional "overdrive in fifth-speed" transmissions were also available. *Lon Arbegust Collection*

"For concrete mixers, excavating and other service where the traction, floatation and load capacity of the six-wheeler are desired [the] Model 622 is available with the tandem-drive Eaton-Hendrickson 28M rear bogie, and with the Timken SLD and SLDD double reduction tandems." The "28M rear bogie" consisted of "two spiral bevel axles in a rocking beam suspension which maintains exact spacing and alignment of axles while permitting complete freedom of individual axle and wheel movement up or down. An inter-axle differential is incorporated in the torque divider with power-operated lockout, providing positive traction when required. [The] Timken SLD and SLDD are larger, of greater capacity, employ double reduction drive and Timken suspension." The SLDD had an inner-axle differential. The tandem axle Model 622's featured 3-speed auxiliary transmissions and frame inner liners as standard equipment. The sales brochure for the Model 622 featured the truck's brakes, declaring, "Diamond T pioneered the use of hydraulic brakes for the heavy-duty truck industry more than twenty years ago. It is natural that brakes of the Model 622 represent the highest development of modern hydraulic systems. Standard braking mechanism is of the latest Wagner FR design with two actuating cylinders at each wheel, providing 'servo' action and uniform pressures for all contact areas of both shoes alike." *Lon Arbegust Collection*

"Here is the 'fruit of several years' hard work by Diamond T engineers. It's a brilliant new series of ultra-modern Heavy-Duty Diamond T's designed to outperform all other trucks of their size and weight ever built. That's a flat statement with no exceptions. It means fuel economy as well as sustained road speed, and taking stiff grades 'in high.' The 162 horse-power Models 660, 720, and 722 are new, from bumper to taillight." This advertising copy from the December 1950 *Commercial Car Journal* announced Diamond T's newest models. This came one year from the introduction of the 1950 "Super-Service" models in December 1949. Diamond T sales literature promoted the many new features of the Model 720, shown above. The new models featured a new 69-inch wide cab supplied by International Harvester. "Probably every modern truck cab is intended to provide safety, comfort, convenience and durability so far as possible. In most cases the product falls measurably short, being limited by the designer's abilities or the necessity of building to a price. For [the] Model 720 however, Diamond T provides a new DeLuxe Cab with one-piece curved windshield which is built with little consideration for cost limitations, and is generally conceded to establish a new standard for the entire industry." *Lon Arbegust Collection*

"Diamond T Diesels are 'Tops' because they're <u>engineered</u> to the job! Shrewd operators are buying Diamond T diesels. They appreciate that reliability and long life assured by Diamond T's engineering each truck precisely to its job." To illustrate this advertising claim in the July 1951 *Commercial Car Journal*, Diamond T featured a photo of "one of four 921-Series Diesels in the service of Jaeger Sand and Gravel Co." The tractor shown above is another of the four. A 743-ci 200 HP Cummins HB-600 diesel powered the Model 921. Diamond T sales material noted the radiator grille "can serve as an individual example of doing the job the *best* way instead of the usual way. It is built up, permitting ready replacement of any damaged part or unit, and the material is <u>permanent stainless steel</u>. Not the cheap appearance of painted stampings, not brittle die castings with a superficial finish of chrome, but an enduring fine appearance. Owners tell us that their older Diamond T's polish up 'like new' even after six and eight years of service on the road." The bumper "was a full 8" in depth and of solid quarter inch stock, [for] real front end protection." *Lon Arbegust Collection*

"Diamond T style adds a *plus* value. No one finishes trucks as painstakingly or as well as Diamond T." The Model 921BR shown above has a front axle set back 11 1/2 inches from the basic position. A 6-cylinder 743-ci 175 HP Cummins HRBB-600 diesel powered the Model 921BR. A 6-cylinder 743-ci 200 HP Cummins NHB-600 powered the Model 921N. According to Diamond T sales material, the 921N was "generally favored for [the] Pacific Coast and Rocky Mountain areas, [while the] 921R [was] fully adequate to most requirements in the rest of the United States." It was also noted, "For the basic tractor models, standard specifications call for the combination of Timken R-100 single-speed rear axle and Fuller 10B1120 ten-speed transmission, which is favored by many operators; the other common choice is the Eaton 20,500 two speed axle with the Spicer 8251A 5-speed transmission." Other options including tandem rear axles were available. Diamond T emphasized the "DeLuxe full-vision safety steel cab." It was also equipped with "Two individual cab seats and back cushions. Both seats are luxuriously upholstered with full Marshall springs throughout and four-layer cushion top construction with foam rubber seat pads covered with heavy 31 oz. calf grain vinyl plastic. A single full width seat is also available for three-man operation when desired." *Lon Arbegust Collection*

"Now, more than ever, is the time to buy Diamond T Quality! The trucks you buy today may have to keep going years longer than usual. And that means just one thing: you should get the *best* trucks money can buy. Buy quality! Get trucks that are built to perform faithfully, economically and profitably year after year for hundreds of thousands of miles." It was April 1951 and the truck shown above illustrated the *Commercial Car Journal* advertisement that featured the quoted copy. The Korean War that began in June 1950 showed no sign of ending soon. As a result, Diamond T decided to tell potential customers that the truck they bought "may have to keep going years longer than usual." Shown at the Chicago Stock Yards, this unidentified tractor may be a Diamond T Model 660, one of the "new heavy-duty series" models introduced in December 1950. The Model 660 was "designed exclusively for tractor-trailer highway service normally carried on 10.00 tires." A 7-bearing 162 HP Diamond T-Continental T-6427 engine powered the Model 660. The standard "heavy-duty single-speed full-floating spiral bevel" rear axle featured a "one-piece forged banjo housing of heat-treated steel." An optional two-speed rear axle was also available. *Lon Arbegust Collection*

"In high-mileage highway service, accessibility is a matter of major importance; accessibility for inspection, adjustment, for routine maintenance and repair. The entire chassis of Model 660 was designed and laid out with this in mind, and Diamond T's exclusive 'Quick-Detachable' front fenders are rated by Service Managers and mechanics as one of the important advances in simplifying their work." This unique feature allowed the entire fender assembly—fender, shield, braces, and headlight—to be removed in "just five to seven minutes." The first step was to detach the headlight wiring system at the junction block. Next, two mechanics would remove the fender mounting bolts that attached to the frame through fender mounting blocks. The third and final step was to lift and set aside the fender assembly. The whole side of the engine was now accessible for maintenance. Diamond T sales material noted this feature saved 20 percent in time and cost, concluding that "In long-distance hauling, the original cost of equipment is properly secondary to the cost of keeping it in service, and the Diamond T design makes for better work as well as for faster servicing." All of this was part of Diamond T's "45-year old policy of taking pains for perfection." *Lon Arbegust Collection*

Commercial Car Journal, March 1952 called the Model 950 and companion Model 951 the "Diamond T Giant." The tractor shown above with Budd wheels probably was equipped with the optional 18,000-pound capacity Schuler FE-18 front axle. Six rear axle options were available. The 36,000-pound capacity "bevel drive" Eaton 36M tandem axle was available with a cast steel housing and also an aluminum housing and aluminum hubs with Budd wheels. The weight reduction was 500 pounds. In addition, three worm drive Timken axles—the 36,000-pound capacity SW3456, the 32,000-pound SW3458, and the 50,000-pound capacity SW456—and two double reduction drive axles—the 50,000-pound capacity SFD4600 and SFDD4600 were offered. In addition to the standard Fuller Ten-Speed 10B-1120 transmission, options included the Fuller Ten-Speed Road-Ranger R-950C and the Spicer 8200 and 8000 Series 3-speed auxiliary transmissions. *Commercial Car Journal* also noted, "These giant diesels have a flat front, a massive cast radiator and brush guard replacing the usual stainless-steel grille." The new 69-inch wide Full-Vision Safety Cab, supplied by International Harvester, was dwarfed by the larger hood. The Bumper-to-Back-of-Cab (BBC) dimension of 127 3/4 inches compared to 110 inches for the Model 720, 116 1/8 inches for the flat front radiator and 121 1/2 inches for the stainless steel grille Model 921s. Frame height, loaded at the front axle, was 37 inches with 10.00 x 20 tires to 40 1/4 inches with 12.00 x 24 tires. *Lon Arbegust Collection*

"F. Wills, road builder, writes to Diamond T. Gentlemen: I am the proud owner of four Diamond T dump trucks, Model 730, XL450 motor, dual drive built up to Diamond T specifications. The Model 730 truck does a fine job in the field on heavy construction." Diamond T's response to potential customers was "Maybe you'd like performance like Mr. Wills gets. See your Diamond T dealer." Testimonials like this could have convinced Tews Ready-Mix concrete. Available in 1953, the Model 730 shown above was equipped with the optional Timken SQDD dual drive tandem rear axle. This axle featured two double-reduction drive axles with an inter-axle differential and manual lock-out. GVW ratings varied with the service from "preferred" at 40,000 to "severe and tractor" at 34,000 pounds. The "massive frame of high-tensile steel" measured 10 x 3 1/2 x 1/4 inches with at least four cross members. "Six-wheelers" featured frame inner-liners over the tandem axles. A 6-cylinder 451-ci 182 HP Hercules-manufactured Diamond T Model XL-450 powered the Model 730. Diamond T sales material noted the instrument panel represented "new convenience. Instruments and controls are grouped for easy reading and manipulating—and they're easily removed from the instrument panel for servicing." *Lon Arbegust Collection*

L.A. Keegstra Produce selected the DeLuxe Sleeper Cab version of Diamond T's 69-inch wide Full-Vision Safety Steel Cab. The Sleeper Cab added 24 inches in length and 85 1/2 inches in width to accommodate the 75 1/2- x 24-inch sleeper compartment. It featured "an extra window on each side of safety glass" a "large luggage storage compartment," and a 6-inch "innerspring mattress of 'Spring-Air' construction." This cab weighed 1050 pounds compared to 500 pounds for the regular cab. Diamond T sales information noted the "Cab suspension is unique in the heavy-duty field. Actually, cab, cowl, hood and radiator (in its 'horse collar' mounting) are trussed together as a single rigid unit. This is flexibly mounted to the frame at four points…. At each of these points a rubber cushion and hold-down spring provide secure anchorage, but cab and sheet metal are isolated from the stresses due to frame distortion. The entire unit is 'floated' and unaffected by extremes of front axle twisting even in the roughest service." While not identified the tractor shown above is probably a 22,000-pound GVW Model 662, introduced in 1955. A 6-cylinder 451-ci 182 HP Diamond T-Hercules manufactured XL-450 powered the tractor. Brakes were "Full air, Westinghouse type" with hydraulic brakes optional. *Lon Arbegust Collection*

Albert Renk, Tacoma, Washington, selected this Model 921N powered by a 6-cylinder 743-ci 200 HP Cummins diesel engine "generally favored for Pacific Coast and Rocky mountain areas." Diamond T sales material pointed out that "Cummins diesels are famous for performance, reliability and economy." Among its features was the "counterbalanced crankshaft [of] a special heavy steel forging with seven main bearings, and Tocco-hardened journals 4 1/2" in diameter. [A] viscous vibration damper is standard equipment, eliminating torsional vibration almost completely." Renk had his choice of four tandem rear axles. The 45,000-pound GVW full floating hypoid bevel Eaton-Hendrickson 36M featured the Hendrickson suspension system that used two rocking beams to distribute the load "exactly 50-50 to the two axles under all conditions [and to] maintain accurate spacing and alignment of axles regardless of wheel movement and relative tire position." The 45,000-pound GVW worm drive Timken SW3022, the similar but greater capacity 50,000-pound Timken SW456, and a double reduction 50,000-pound GVW Timken SDF460 was also available. "In Timken tandems the functions of axle alignment and spacing and load carrying are clearly separated. Long resilient leaf springs divide the load equally between driving axles, but spring ends are not attached to axle housings. Eight rubber mounted torque arms...absorb all torque loads and maintain the axles in parallel position." *Lon Arbegust Collection*

"The Truck of Lowest Cost" appeared at the bottom of each Diamond T advertisement for the new Heavy-Duty models. While new from "bumper to tail light," Diamond T did not mention style as it had in its pre-World War II advertising. Reliability, efficiency, and low cost operation were the appeals made to customers like the McJunkin Supply Company. The Model 720, shown above, featured an "Eaton 18501 full floating 2-speed bevel [rear axle], with second reduction for the low-speed range through planetary gears." Optional Diamond T Vari-Rate rear springs, promoted as providing an "almost unbelievably better ride," weighed 280-300 pounds less than other systems. According to Diamond T sales information "the spring proper is exceptionally long and deeply cambered. In the no-load position, it contacts the frame hangers only at the extreme tips…. Then, as load is applied, the spring flattens out, and the effective length reduces. The inner face of the hangers has a cam-shaped curvature, so that spring length and stiffness are always exactly proportioned to the load." Diamond T literature also noted "The Westinghouse air-brake system is favored by practically all operators for heavy-duty trucks, and is supplied as standard equipment on Model 720, regardless of the size or type of rear axle that is specified." *Lon Arbegust Collection*

"The Newest and Highest Development of the Cab-over-Engine Design. DIAMOND T's TILT-CAB models embody an entirely new technique in Cab-over-Engine design. No essential change is made from the conventional engine, clutch, transmission, frame, axles, and other major elements, which are the tried and tested Diamond T units familiar to truck operators throughout the world. However, Diamond T engineers have combined these units into a full Cab-over-Engine vehicle, in which the cab, by an ingenious system of counterbalances, tilts forward for servicing without the need of a power unit of any kind." As this quotation indicates, Diamond T took great pride in the new COE tilt cab models introduced in 1953. The earliest versions of these models featured the Diamond T emblem on the door as shown in the Model 422C tractor in the above photograph. By 1954, photographs show the emblem on the cab behind the door. To tilt the cab the operator first released the clamp lock lever on the back of the cab. Second, the inside-the-cab safety release latch was pulled. For added safety, this latch only worked with the cab door open. The operator would then "gently" lift the cab by the rear of the fender. Counterbalancing coil springs "actually [did] the actual lifting." A final step was to position a strut rod to prevent accidental lowering of the cab. *Lon Arbegust Collection*

Diamond T Tilt-Cab models were initially offered in three series. According to the *Commercial Car Journal*, September 1953 the Model 422C and 422CH covered the "general range of city delivery service with GVW ratings from 17,000 to 22,000 lb." A 6-cylinder 271-ci 112 HP Continental K-6271 engine supplied the power. "For heavier loads and higher speeds on the highway," the Model 522C and Model 622C provide GVW ratings of 17,500 to 26,000 pounds. A 330-ci 141 HP Continental K-6330 engine powered the Model 522, while a 363-ci 150 HP Continental K-6363 supplied power to the Model 622C series. Diamond T added "C" to Cab-over-Engine models and an "H" for models with heavy-duty rear axles. The models were offered in seven wheelbase options. These ranged from 93 inches for the tractor shown above, to 99, 111, 123, 129, 147, and 159 inches. The cab featured two 33- x 26-inch windshield sections. The "nearly horizontal" steering wheel was designed to "reduce steering effort because the normal pull of the driver's arm is perpendicular to the wheel rim." The cooling system featured a 690 square inch radiator, cushion mounted to isolate it from frame distortion. The cab grille was a "permanent mold aluminum casting." The 60,000-pound GVW diesel powered Model 723C was introduced in 1954. *Lon Arbegust Collection*

The Model 723CJT, "Diamond T's hottest!" The December 19, 1956 *Diamond T Sales Bulletin* was devoted exclusively to the "Tilt-Cab turbodiesel which is smashing existing records right and left." The coverage included the above photograph and comments by R.T. "Bob" Herrin, President of Herrin Transportation Company of Houston, Texas, who stated "flatly that 723CJT is '*THE tractor for profitable over-the-road operations.*'" The Herrin fleet consisted of forty-eight Model 723CJT's with several million total miles logged. According to the *Bulletin*, "Average fuel mileage of the 48 Tilt-Cab diesels to date is a thrifty 7.3 miles per gallon. This money saving mileage is coupled with a GVW of 58,420 pounds." The 723CJT "chalked up two bonus advantages for Herrin, in addition to the drastic slash in fuel costs—a savings in trailer loading time and an increase in payload. The Tilt-Cab design itself permits of more revenue-producing payload per unit, since more weight is carried on the front axle. Dock time has been trimmed and handling of freight simplified because it can be loaded faster with assurance that legal axle loads will not be exceeded." As the "only Tilt-Cab diesel tractor with 60-inch front springs and Variable-Rate rear springs," Diamond T stressed driver comfort. *Detroit Public Library, National Automotive History Collection*

"'Costs overwhelmingly in favor of Diamond T…now converting our entire fleet.' Why? ANO's president T.S. Johnson tells you. 'The results of our exhaustive six-month study of equipment and maintenance costs were overwhelmingly in favor of our twelve Diamond T's. Their standout performance has forced us to make a change. *We are now converting our entire fleet of eighty over-the-road trucks to these Diamond T model 830s.*'" Diamond T featured a photograph similar to that shown above along with this advertising copy in the January 1957, *Commercial Car Journal.* The advertisement continued with additional comments by T.S. Johnson, ANO's—Atlanta-New Orleans Motor Freight Company—President. "'We are getting better than five miles per gallon and the 830's operate between 120,000 and 140,000 miles before we have to go into the engine. Our overall down time and maintenance cost is way below any other truck of like capacity in the fleet we are converting.' Your operation may not be similar to ANO. But every Diamond T is 'custom built'—to match your particular hauling needs." A 6-cylinder 501-ci Hercules-manufactured XL-501 engine powered the Model 830. The advertisement featured the slogan, first used in 1956, "The Diamond is for Quality." *Detroit Public Library, National Automotive History Collection*

"The Diamond T Tilt-Cab design of Model 921C is the product of years of development to provide the most efficient vehicle for the transport of maximum legal loads. It provides the specific advantage of a unique combination of compact dimensions, light weight and instant accessibility, plus the performance and economy of Cummins diesel engines in a range to 300 horsepower." The counterbalanced aluminum cab tilted manually. The curved-face cab was 71 inches bumper-to-back-of-cab (BBC) and 89 3/4 inches wide. The "huge" 1,880 square inch twin windshield was the "largest in any highway vehicle." Barely visible in the above photograph behind the diesel exhaust stack is the sleeper extension. While adding only 13 inches to the overall length of the cab, it provided a 24-inch wide berth equipped with a 4 1/2-inch "air-foam mattress." During its production, the Model 923C offered a variety of supercharged and non-supercharged 6-cylinder Cummins diesel engines. *Commercial Car Journal*, March 1958, carried an article about the Model 900CHS powered by a 590-ci 239 HP Hall Scott Spartan Model 590 gasoline engine. This engine weighed 1275 pounds, almost a half ton less than diesel engines of equal power. Diamond T touted the extra payload capacity and also offered a Hall Scott LPG engine. *Lon Arbegust Collection*

"The genii touch comes to trucking. Announcing Diamond T Presto-Matic. A button (believe it or not) replaces the clutch pedal…eliminates clutch pedal fatigue!" Advertising in the January 1959 *Commercial Car Journal*, Diamond T explained its "new semi-automatic transmission system" available on diesels such as the Model 921FR shown above. The ad explained, "This exclusive Diamond T bonus is a low cost option with Spicer 5-speed and 12-speed synchro-mesh transmissions and 2-plate clutches. Best of all it is driver controlled. A mere touch of the finger activates the Diamond T Presto-Matic. Smooth engagement from a standing start is automatic. A sensing mechanism synchronizes the action of the clutch to engine speed, exactly as an expert driver would if using a pedal. Full engagement is effected before the engine builds up to maximum torque. When the engine returns to idling speed the clutch is automatically disengaged. The combination of these two automatic actions enables a driver to inch along in heavy traffic—without ever touching the control or shifting gears, just as he would with a fully-automatic transmission." The configuration of the tractor shown above indicates the possible use of a dromedary or "drom" cargo box between the cab and the semi-trailer for additional "cube" or payload capacity. *Lon Arbegust Collection*

"No other truck ever built matches the New Diamond T Diesel 923." First featured in an article in the January 1, 1958 *Commercial Car Journal*, the 29,000-pound GVW Model 923 featured a new 672-ci 180 HP Cummins HF-6-B diesel engine. It was available with the traditional Diamond T "Streamline radiator shell with [chrome bar] grille and ornament" or a flat front radiator with cast aluminum tanks. A front axle set forward for "bridge formula" states and a set-back front axle were optional configurations. In 1959, following its acquisition by the White Motor Company, Diamond T began to offer the "D" Series featuring the "D" cab, based on the Autocar Driver Cab, first introduced in 1950. This 72-inch wide cab replaced the 69-inch wide "Full-Vision Safety-Steel Cab" manufactured by International Harvester. Gone were the hood louvers, replaced by three chrome spears flowing from the Diamond T emblem. While not identified, the truck in the above photograph may be a new "D" Series Model 923D. Diamond T offered eight optional tandem rear axles. Maximum GVW ratings for six-wheelers ranged from 41,000 pounds for models equipped with the Timken SLHD to 55,000 pounds for models with the Eaton 42M tandem rear axle. The same engine powered the new Model 923. Cummins had revised its engine designations, so that the previous HF-6-B was now the NH-180. *Lon Arbegust Collection*

"Diamond T Quality is Not Conversation—Compare specifications before you buy! Every Diamond T diesel, of course, is custom-built to the job. There is a choice of 6 engines, 12 main transmissions, 6 auxiliaries, 11 rear axles, 12 tandems, 3 positions for front axle, etc. This is desirable, even necessary, but not unique. It is in the rigid quality standards of basic specifications that Diamond T cannot be matched." Diamond T used its August 1959 *Commercial Car Journal* advertisement to promote the new "D" Series diesels "built with 10" frame siderails of heat-treated chrome-nickel molybdenum steel—tensile strength 105,000 lbs. per sq. in. This is a higher quality—and higher cost—frame material than is used by anyone else in the industry, so far as we know." The 30,000 to 41,000 pound GVW Model 921 DFN shown above featured a "set-forward front axle," 29 7/8" back of the front bumper. The "F" models featured "extra capacity" radiators with "top tanks and side members of cast aluminum, buffed and polished." Radiator shutters were standard. Other components that highlighted Diamond T's emphasis on quality included a Hopkins lightweight muffler, hydraulic shock absorbers, front tow pins, and stainless steel hood trim. *Lon Arbegust Collection*

"Do Diamond T Trucks Last Longer? Absolutely. Diamond Ts last longer because every truck is custom built to match the job. Exactly." A companion model to the axle forward Model 921DF, the 30,000 to 41,000 pound range GVW Model 921DB shown above was designed to "permit maximum gross loads on the highway." It was capable of hauling "40 ft. or longer semi-trailers or combinations comfortably within a 55 ft. overall length limit." The Model 921DB featured a "Set-back front axle [that] allows maximum transfer of weight forward, providing more equalized distribution of weight to axles where the 'bridge formula' does not apply." The distance from the front bumper to the centerline of the front axle was 48 1/2 inches. The companion Model 921DF featured a flat front radiator and the front axle set forward. This configuration "provided the most favorable chassis dimensions for maximum highway loads in states where the 'bridge formula' applies. (Under 'bridge formula' gross weights can be increased to a specific maximum as the distance between extreme front and rear axles increases.)" Diamond T offered a lightweight version of each of these models. The Model 922DB saved 150 pounds on the 4x2 and 300 pounds on the 6x4 versions. The Model 922DF saved 100 and 200 pounds on the 4x2 and 6x4 models, respectively. *Lon Arbegust Collection*

"Get total 'Payformance'…get Diamond T. Since 1905 Diamond T has rolled up millions of more profitable miles for its owners. Its record for earnings and longevity is unexcelled. Whatever your job requirements demand, you can expect total 'Payformance' from Diamond T. Its resale value is unequalled. Today's Diamond T is the product of this money-making history. That means higher earning power and lower cost-per-mile, more payload, and less maintenance. Your investment in a Diamond T is by far the most profitable one you can make." The "extra lightweight" 42,000 to 76,000-pound GVW Model 922 DF, shown above, was in a Diamond T sales brochure to validate these marketing statements. It featured a "special flat front radiator and front axle set forward." A lightweight aluminum version of the "D" cab reduced cab weight by 250 pounds. While retaining the "girder-type construction…the frame panels, and floorboard mountings are aluminum." An optional 80-inch wide sleeper cab featured a 75x24-inch berth-type bed behind the seats. The "innerspring mattress" rested on a 4-inch box spring. The 142-inch BBC sleeper cab was 22 1/2 inches longer than the regular "D" cab. When introduced in August 1959, these models offered Cummins and Detroit diesel engines, nine transmissions, eleven rear axle and four front axle options. *Lon Arbegust Collection*

Nearly every Diamond T advertisement was a testimonial, with a satisfied customer's truck shown in a brief "photo-op" while at work. "Sweetest thing on the road," said T.E. Burleson, who used his "D" Series Diamond T to haul honey. The 1961 ad continued, "Diamond T economy and long life is an old story with Burleson—some of his units are still going strong after the million-mile mark." Another advertisement exclaimed "6.3 m.p.g. with 60,000 lbs. GCW…Diamond T Diesels are Money Makers! That's from the records of The J.M. Smucker Co. No ifs ands or buts. The figures prove Diamond T diesels cut costs." Perhaps such ads prompted Nelson Dykgraaf officials to purchase their Model 931B. According to Diamond T sales information, the "Exclusive cast aluminum radiator is standard with capacity increased to meet cooling requirements of high output engines." The dimension from the front bumper to the center of the front axle on the model shown was 43 1/2 inches with a BBC of 119 1/2 inches. "F" models, with the axle forward, measured 28 and 119 1/2 inches respectively. Nelson Dykgraaf opted for a detached sleeper box. The 22 1/2-inch longer "D" sleeper cab Diamond T offered was 80 inches wide at the rear with a "large luggage compartment" beneath the bed accessible through doors on each side of the cab. *Lon Arbegust Collection*

Commercial Car Journal, March 1959 introduced the 31,500 pound GVW Model 931C shown above. "The compact 931C is designed for reduced chassis weight, and the short 50-in. bumper-to-back-of-cab (BBC) dimension permits pulling maximum length semi-trailers—also 25-ft [to 27-foot] doubles in western states. Bumper-to-front axle dimension is 28 in. favorable for maximum loads under 'bridge formula' restrictions." The bridge formula refers to the equalization of the load on each of a truck's axles. Diamond T advertising emphasized the three versions of the new Cab-Over-Engine design. "A choice of three cabs in the 931C means the right cab for any operation. The basic 931C has a 50-inch two-man cab. Sleeper cabs include a 25-inch 'bustle-back' version...and a full-skirted sleeper cab [shown above] with a 30-inch berth. BBC on the full-skirted cab is 80 inches." The Model 931C compared favorably with the "flat face" Freightliners introduced starting in 1953. The Freightliner Spacemaker was 48 inches BBC, but featured a "pancake" or horizontally mounted engine located under the frame and behind the cab. Later Freightliner models with engine configurations similar to the Diamond T Model 931C measured 75 inches BBC with a smaller sleeper cab. The "mostly aluminum, fully-insulated" Diamond T cab was 89 1/4 inches overall in width. *Lon Arbegust Collection*

"Kroehler loads 60 bulky sofas and 60 matching chairs. Diamond T builds the Tilt-cab Diesel." This headline, from the February 1960 *Commercial Car Journal* Diamond T advertisement highlighted the photograph of the Model 931C shown above. The ad continued noting, "Uncrated furniture is bulky, fragile and prone to 'rubs.' Hauling 60 sofas and 60 matching chairs per load takes a rig with maximum cube as well as 'trucking know-how.' Kroehler Manufacturing Company, world's largest furniture maker (and owner of one of the nation's largest private truck fleets), does the job at rock-bottom cost. A sleeper cab is needed because this unit operates on a turn-around basis." Kroehler specified a 25-inch "bustle-back" sleeper compartment rather than the 30-inch deep "full-skirted" sleeper compartment enabling them "to haul two 27 ft. doubles within the legal train length of 65 ft." The "bustle back" sleeper did not cover the entire rear of the cab. Diamond T initially offered five 6-cylinder Cummins diesel engines for the Model 931C ranging from the 672-ci 180 HP NH-180 to the supercharged 262 HP 695-ci NTO-6. The Model 931C featured a "hydraulic tilting, self-latching cab," that allowed "access to the entire radiator-engine-transmission area, facilitating inspection and service work of any kind."
Lon Arbegust Collection

Diamond T sales literature promoted the features of the Model 931C cab. "Drivers like 931C cabs. The driver sits high above the road in a commanding position; vision is extraordinarily good. The two huge windshields are of Solex safety plate glass, glare-absorbing and heat-reducing. Door windows are crank controlled, and include a large ventilating wing forward section, with stainless steel framing. [The] steering wheel is positioned and angled for maximum efficiency and leverage. All instruments, including tachometer, are directly in front of the driver. Appointments are unusually complete, [and] include dual heavy-duty windshield wipers, two bus-type rear view mirrors, two 5" side-view mirrors, two sun visors, glove compartment, windshield washers, cigar lighter. Oversize fresh air heating system optional; keeps windshield clear even in sub-zero temperatures." Important, too, was driver comfort. The driver's seat was the "Bostrom torsion-spring 'Westcoaster,' with a Bostrom light-weight companion seat." The driver's seat was pedestal mounted and adjustable horizontally and vertically and for the driver's weight. "Plastic-treated foam rubber" insulated the engine housing, cab sides, back, and floor. An access door on the housing permitted servicing "water and oil without raising the cab." The sleeper cabs were equipped with 4 1/2-inch "air foam" mattresses. *Lon Arbegust Collection*

"The 931C is the product of Diamond T's years of experience in building diesel powered Tilt-cab tractors. It is designed to transport maximum legal loads over the road at the lowest possible cost per mile." The quality of the components Diamond T selected for the Model 931C reflected its "years of experience." These included an 11,000-pound capacity Timken FE-900 front axle and a variety of 23,000-pound capacity Timken and Eaton rear axles. Options for "six-wheelers" included Timken and Eaton Tandem rear axles with capacities that ranged from 34,000 to 38,000 pounds. Transmissions were available in a number of configurations. Options included the 5-speed, constant-mesh helical gear Fuller 5C72 and 5C720; the Fuller R96 and R960 10-speed RoadRanger; and the synchromesh, single lever control Spicer 8125 12-speed transmission. Cummins NH, NRT, and NT series diesels including turbo-charged and super-charged models with displacements from 672- to 855-ci and horsepower ratings from 195 to 335. Engines of 280 HP and up powered for "six-wheelers." Diamond T specified Spicer 14-inch and 15 1/2-inch 2-plate clutches, matched to specific engines. The Delco Remy electrical system featured a 12 volt, 50 amp. gear driven generator and four 6 volt, 150 amp. hrs. capacity batteries. *Lon Arbegust Collection*

"New! Fiberglass Tilt-Cab from Diamond T! Safer, longer-lived, lighter, quieter, more comfortable!" This headline and the photograph of the Model 634CG shown above were featured in Diamond T's May 1960, *Commercial Car Journal* advertisement. According to the advertisement, "Diamond T's new fiberglass Tilt-cab defies age, needs practically no maintenance because it cannot rust or corrode. Fiberglass construction cuts cab weight 360 lbs., which means more payload, lower costs per ton-mile and more profit!" The ad continued with a typographical error. "Fiberglass is almost incredibly strong and durable." It would seem that "almost" should have been "also." Continuing, the ad notes "Tensile strength of individual glass fibers is of the order of 20,000 lbs. per square inch, and the resilient fiberglass compound has an impact resistance greater than 1020 steel. It is practically impossible to dent or produce permanent set in fiberglass. The driver is safer in the Diamond T fiberglass Tilt-cab because of the cushioning effect of the material. He's more comfortable, too. Fiberglass has a pronounced insulating quality so that the cab is warmer in winter, cooler in summer, and quieter by far at all times. The cab will retain its rugged strength and gleaming glass-smooth finish for years. The grille featured chrome bars reflecting the design of other Diamond Ts." *Detroit Public Library, National Automotive History Collection*

"New from Diamond T…gas jobs that live longer, cost less to own and to run." This February 1961 headline in *Commercial Car Journal* featured a photograph of a Model 4300 "six wheeler," similar to the truck shown above, but loaded with lumber. According to Diamond T sales literature, complementing the Reo or "R" cab was the "Streamline radiator shell and ornament [and] grille faced with stainless steel." The grille featured ribbed bars, a Diamond T feature since the 1930s, with this particular design based on styling introduced in 1952. The Model 4300 series featured a "Four piece, pressed-steel hood" and dual headlights, also popular on cars at the time, were integrated into the new style "heavy gauge fenders." The 4300 Series featured the 42,000-pound GVW Model 4300, the 43,000-pound GVW Model 4320, and the 47,000-pound "special extra capacity Mixer Truck Package Model 4360." For mixer trucks an optional "Flywheel-power-take-off" saved 200 to 600 lbs. in weight. A geared belt drove the output shaft directly from the crankshaft. A Super-Service Reo-built 331-ci 170 HP 6-cylinder DT6-170 or an optional 185 HP 362-ci DT6-185 powered the 4300 Series Models. Available tandem rear axles included the standard 34,000 pound capacity Timken SLHD and the optional 34,000-pound Eaton 32M. *Michigan State University Archives and Historical Collections*

"The Diamond T concept—every truck 'custom built' to match the job—exactly! Basic, isn't it? Trucks dealt 'off-the-shelf' are pretty sure to cost more in the long run. They must be built to 'averages'—and very few truck jobs are average." A wide range of rear axles were among the components that reflected the "custom built" concept for the Diamond T 5000 Series model, introduced in January 1961, shown above. A 22,400-pound Eaton 1893 full floating spiral bevel rear axle was standard. Options included planetary, hypoid, and double reduction rear axles from Timken and Eaton. In October 1959, *Commercial Car Journal* covered the introduction of three new Diamond T models that featured the Reo-based "R" cab and Reo-built "Super-Service" engines. The 5000 Series featured the "R" cab. The Super-Service 170 HP 331-ci 6-cylinder DT6-170 was standard with a 185 HP 362-ci 6-cylinder DT6-185 available as an option. The 29,000-pound GVW Model 5000 featured a 9,000-pound "drop forged I-beam section" Timken FD-901 front axle. With the optional 11,000-pound Timken FE-900 oversize front axle, the model designation became 5020 and the GVW rating increased to 31,000 pounds. The design of the 30-gallon fuel tanks provided steps for easier cab access. *Michigan State University Archives and Historical Collections*

"The engine is the heart of the truck, and no truck can be better than its engine." Following the acquisition of Diamond T by the White Motor Company in 1958, sharing of components among other truck brands acquired by White began. White had acquired Reo in 1957, and the 1961 Diamond T 5300 Series, shown above, featured the Reo-based cab introduced in 1939 and Reo Gold Comet engines. Diamond T identified these as Super-Service engines with a "DT6" designation. The standard engine in the 48,000-pound GVW Model 5300 was the 6-cylinder 331-ci 170 HP Super-Service DT6-170. An extra cost option was the 6-cylinder 362-ci 185 HP Super-Service DT6-185. One feature of this engine Diamond T emphasized was the "best cooling system in the business," explaining that "more than 90 gallons of water per minute flow through the system." In addition, "Water from the block is forced up into the cylinder head to strategically located nozzle jets which direct the cooling flow at the valve seat areas." A 52,000-pound GVW Model 5360 "Mixer Truck Package" was available. It featured a heavier Timken front axle, extra-capacity springs, larger size front tires, a full air brake system and Ross HPS power steering. Timken SQD and SQDD double reduction 38,000-pound capacity rear axles were also options. *Michigan State University Archives and Historical Collections*

115

"Pilot picks Diamond T Diesel 990. More Cube—More Weight—More—Freight." This headline ran under the above photograph in Diamond T's October 1961, *Commercial Car Journal* advertisement. Introduced in August 1960, the 30,000-pound GVW Model 990 featured a 90-inch bumper-to-back-of-cab (BBC) dimension allowing hauling of 40-foot "square-nose trailers" with an overall length under 50 feet, accommodating states with a 50-foot length limit. Because of its compact size, the Model 990's engine intruded into the cab. "Removal of the 990's quick-detachable fender (in less than six minutes) and the fiberglass engine compartment cover lets mechanics walk right in to the entire under-hood area." The Model 990 featured the "D" cab. This 72-inch wide all-steel cab was the Autocar Driver Cab, first introduced by Autocar in 1950. White Motor Company, now the owner of Diamond T, also offered Diamond T models equipped with Reo ("R") cabs and engines. A 6-cylinder 190 HP 743-ci HRF-6 Cummins diesel was standard on the eighty 4x2 Model 990's owned by Pilot Freight Carriers, Inc., Winston Salem, N.C. Other Cummins diesel options included two 743-ci engines: the 195 HP NHE-195 (standard on the 6x4s), the 220 HP NH-220, and two 855-ci engines, the 225 HP NHE-225 and the 250 HP NH-250. *Detroit Public Library, National Automotive History Collection*

116

By November 1962, Diamond T Model 990 advertising in *Commercial Car Journal* emphasized lightweight construction for more payload revenue. "For example…an aluminum cab. Aluminum radiator tanks. Aluminum cross-members. Aluminum battery box, fuel tanks—but the list could go on and on." Diamond T sales literature featured the above photograph. The 30,000-pound GVW tractor featured a "Gleaming polished aluminum radiator [that] dissipates heat rapidly, can't rust. Over-size core area (840 sq. in.) easily cools big diesels even in the hottest climates." The four-piece hood assembly was also aluminum. Later, Diamond T added additional engines for the Model 990: the 180 HP 6-cylinder 672-ci Cummins NH-180 and NHE-180. All Cummins engines used by Diamond T featured an aluminum flywheel housing, timing gear cover, oil pan, and intake manifold. A wide range of rear axles featured Eaton and Timken spiral bevel, hypoid, double reduction, two-speed and two-speed double reduction options for single rear axle models. An Eaton planetary double reduction axle was an additional option for tandem rear axle models that ranged from 41,000- to 55,000-pound GVW. The 10- x 3 1/2- x 1/4-inch "hi-tensile steel" frame featured a minimum of four cross members. A 134-inch wheelbase was standard with 146-, 182-, and 200-inch lengths optional. *Detroit Public Library, National Automotive History Collection*

"Every Diamond T is 'custom-built.' Engine, transmission, axles and other components are specifically chosen to match the job. In each case Diamond T provides the finest units in the industry…. But in this new 'P' line the basic design provides a further measure of advantage to the operator, with basic dimensions and layout which are particularly favorable in construction work." A *Commercial Car Journal* article covered the new models in November 1962. Ten basic models were offered in the "P" Series, including four 2-axle trucks and tractors, three "tandem-drive six-wheelers, and three all-wheel-drive models—a 2-axle 4x4 series and two series of 6x6 six wheelers." Among the special-purpose vehicles in the "P" line was the "Mixer Truck Package" shown above and available as the Model P4360 and Model P5360. Three Super-Service 6-cylinder Reo Gold Comet-based gas engines were offered. The 170 HP 331-ci DT6-170 was standard with the 186 HP 362-ci DT6-186 and the 200 HP 401-ci DT6-200 optional at extra cost. The optional engines featured extra capacity cooling systems with 150 gallons per minute water circulation and 720 square inch radiators. Two 6 cylinder Cummins diesel engines were available, the 160 HP 464-ci CF-160 and the 180 HP 464-ci C-180. The latter required "Engineering department approval." *Author's Collection*

"Now…the Diamond T All-American Air-Flo 931C. The one best truck design for all American highway operations!" In 1962, Diamond T first offered a modified windshield for the Model 931C, by adding two curved sections on each side, further increasing visibility for the 89 1/4-inch wide cab. In contrast, the "Full Vision" cab, manufactured by International Harvester and used on most models, was 69 inches wide. By 1964, nine Cummins diesel engine options were available, ranging from 190 to 335 horsepower. These included "naturally aspirated, super-charged and turbo-charged sixes, and the powerful V8-265." According to Diamond T sales literature, "Diamond T-Cummins diesels have aluminum gear cover, oil-pan, intake manifold and flywheel housing. Also offered are aluminum battery boxes, fuel tanks, suspension beams and many other weight-reducing options." The advantage of these weight savings was increased payload and as a result, greater profits for the truck user. Naturally aspirated engines utilized a Spicer 14-inch two-plate clutch, while supercharged engines required a two-plate Spicer 15 1/2-inch clutch. Diamond T offered seventeen main transmission options that included 4-speed and 5-speed constant mesh, 5-speed synchro mesh, 10-speed, 12-speed, or 16-speed "compound main transmissions." Five auxiliary transmissions were also available. Nine single and eleven tandem axles offered hypoid, double-reduction, or spiral bevel designs.
Detroit Public Library, National Automotive History Collection

"Ready to whip your toughest calls. Diamond T quality is *custom engineered* into every model in our powerful 'P' Series, and any of these models can be custom engineered to do your job as it should be done! Whether your operation requires a 4x2, 4x4, 6x4, or a 6x6 wheel arrangement, Diamond T can *Custom Engineer* a dependable 'P' Series model to exactly fit your specifications." Available Cummins, Detroit Diesel, and Perkins diesels as well as five gas and three LPG engines provided power. The "P" Series models offered an optional 90-degree tilting hood and fender assembly. "The one-piece hood and fender assembly is of rustproof, salt resistant, fiberglass construction, thus it will not rot or corrode. No fenders to climb on, no hood to work under...." Increased payload was also possible with the 110-pound weight saving. Diamond T featured the above photograph in the "P" Series brochure that also featured the text quoted. Now the Diamond T Motor Truck Division of the White Motor Company, Diamond T's "P" Series clearly reflected White's integration of Diamond T and Reo. In essence, the "P" Series was a Reo with a grille reflecting recognizable Diamond T styling. *Lon Arbegust Collection*

"We could skimp on quality…but then it wouldn't be a Diamond T. We could make it cheaper. Cut back on engineering. Relax production standards. Reduce our rigid quality control. But you wouldn't get the kind of truck you expect from Diamond T. The high-quality, precision-built, able-to-take-it-type truck that comes from Diamond T. And today, from Diamond T, comes the fabulous new Thousand-Line—the ultra lightweight truck that lets you haul hundreds of pounds more payload—FREE. The world's lightest heavy-duty diesel. Built to take it. Built to give it—built to give more profitable 'Payformance.'" Diamond T advertised the new Thousand-Line Series in the May 1965 *Commercial Car Journal*. The 44,000- to 55,000-pound GVW Model 1046FL shown above was a companion to the 33,000- to 34,000-pound GVW 4x2 Model 1044FL. Both models featured aluminum frame rails and cross-members, spring hangers and "hundreds of other parts [that] cut weight but add strength." The hood and fenders were of "tough, resilient U.S. Rubber Royalex, which insulates, sound-proofs, gives ample protection, is easily repaired." The "bolted frame assembly is far stronger than riveted construction, [and] is easier to service and repair." The truck also featured the Autocar-based Driver Cab "D" Cab. *Lon Arbegust Collection*

In the March 1966 *Commercial Car Journal*, Diamond T introduced "The Westerner." Shown above, it was the "newest of the Thousand-Line series" and "the newest and most improved of the lightweight heavies." A restyled grille replaced the familiar Diamond T chrome bar grille on the models introduced in May 1965. The Model 1044 and Model 1046 were available with either steel or 2014-T6 aluminum alloy frame and cross members. The frames featured nut and bolt construction, a practice long utilized by Autocar, acquired by the White Motor Company in 1953. The addition of an "L" to the model designation indicated the use of the aluminum frame. Models with an "F" had a front axle set forward, while a "B" indicated a front axle set back 18 inches. A 90-inch BBC "snub-nosed" Model 1090 was introduced in June 1966. Also available in June was the "C" Series based on the cab-over-engine Model 931C. A 220 HP Cummins NH-220 diesel was standard while ten other optional 6-cylinder and V-8 Cummins, Detroit Diesel, and Caterpillar diesels ranging from 218 to 335 HP powered these models. The 90 degree tilting U.S. Rubber Royalex hood and fender assembly continued as did the use of the Diamond T "D" cab. Diamond T specified Rockwell front and rear axles as well as Rockwell Stopmaster brakes as standard equipment. *Detroit Public Library, National Automotive History Collection*

"Go with The Trend. The modern truck with the Lifetime Cab." Diamond T introduced the 24,000-pound GVW Trend in 1966. According to Diamond T sales material, the revolutionary Lifetime Cab "is made with Royalex, the miracle material that won't rust or corrode. It is completely unaffected by salts, acids, or other rust accelerating chemicals. [It] will look new after years of hard use. The Royalex outer shell of the Lifetime Cab is supported by an extruded aluminum-alloy frame and a heavy steel understructure. [The] doors are galvanized steel with exterior drain holes to prevent water entrapment." Due to the engine location below and behind the cab seats, there was a "clear walk-through aisle with a fully adjustable driver's seat and a full width companion seat for two." A 327-ci 185 HP V-8 engine powered the Trend. The cab also featured the "easiest-to-operate tilt cab on the market. One man does it in seconds by releasing the catch and lifting. Coil springs assist the titling action. With the cab tilted, the entire engine compartment is completely accessible for routine servicing. Battery, radiator fill, dip stick, oil fill, and alternator are all easily reached. Cuts servicing time to a minimum, reduces maintenance costs." Initially, White, Diamond T, and Reo, as well as Oliver and Minneapolis-Moline farm equipment manufacturers, all part of White Motor Corporation, offered the Trend. *Detroit Public Library, National Automotive History Collection*

"The Diamond Reo C-114 Series may be new in name but it's backed by a 125-year old tradition of quality and value. It combines the finest selection of components available today in a conventional model." Introduced in May 1967, the Diamond Reo replaced both Diamond T and Reo. The "125-year old tradition" acknowledged Reo's 63-year history (1904-1967) and Diamond T's 62-year history (1905-1967) of manufacturing cars and trucks. Continuity was the watchword. The Thousand-Line Model 1044 and Model 1046 Diamond Ts were now the C-114 and C-114L, with the "L" models utilizing lightweight aluminum components. The C-90 Series replaced the 90-inch BBC "snub-nosed" Diamond T Model 1090. The Diamond Reo C-101 Series was the new designation for the "P" Series that utilized the "R" or Reo cab. While up-dated and improved over the

years, the cab's basic design dates to 1939. Apart from the new name on the hood assembly and the new emblem above the grille, the new models were virtually identical to the Diamond T models. The only cosmetic change was a different mesh for the grille. Diamond Reo also continued a Tilt-Cab Forward Model CF-83 based on the 422C, 522C, and 622C Series, initially introduced in 1953, and later designated the CG Series. *Detroit Public Library, National Automotive History Collection*

Diamond Reo was ultimately an acknowledgement of the lack of the viability of two distinct brands without distinct products to offer. Diamond Reo continued to offer the Trend. The emphasis in Diamond Reo 1969 sales material for the medium weight field CF-6842 Trend continued to focus on the "Life Time" (now two words) cab made from Uniroyal Synthetic Steel …unaffected by rust or corrosion." The material was identical even though U.S. Rubber was now Uniroyal and Royalex was now "Synthetic Steel." Diamond Reo claimed a $200 savings per year in maintenance costs due to this cab material. Heat from a hair blow dryer was often enough to eliminate any "dents" in the cab material. In addition to the 327-ci 185 HP V-8 gasoline engine Diamond Reo offered an optional 235 HP "high performance" engine. The BBC dimension was 69 inches and the distance from the front axle to the back of the cab

was only 17 inches giving the Trend "a good transfer of weight forward, [resulting] in higher payloads." Diamond Reo noted the Trend was up to 37 inches shorter than a conventional model with the same size body. The turning radius for the highly maneuverable Trend with a 119-inch wheelbase was only 25 feet 4 inches. *Detroit Public Library, National Automotive History Collection*

"With Diamond Reo you never send a 'boy' to do a 'man's' job…you get the <u>right</u> frame, <u>right</u> axles, <u>right</u> suspension!" The Thousand-Line "C" Series models based on the 50-inch BBC cab-over-engine Diamond T Model 931C became the CO-50 and CO-78 (Sleeper) Diesel Series, shown above. Diamond Reo sales material noted these models were "compact, but spacious, with modern streamlined design. [The] deluxe lightweight cab with functional clustering of instruments and switches [featured a] 90 degree tilt cab, hydraulically operated." In an effort to distinguish itself from other manufacturers, Diamond Reo introduced the "Certified Product Reliability Program" at the start of 1968. *Overdrive* magazine covered this inspection and testing program in November 1968. As the trucks moved down the assembly line, the factory service manager kept a watchful eye for defects. At the end of the line, the truck entered a three-stage inspection. The first stage involved a complete inspection by a three-member team with any defects corrected, emblems attached, and wheel balancing completed. The second stage featured a 20-mile road test involving city, "expressway," and rural roads. The final third stage inspection including a water test to check for leaks. The owner received all records with copies kept in Diamond Reo's offices in Lansing, Michigan. *Detroit Public Library, National Automotive History Collection*

More great books from
Iconografix

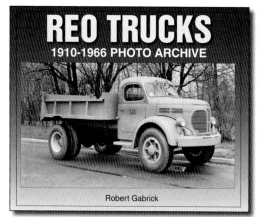
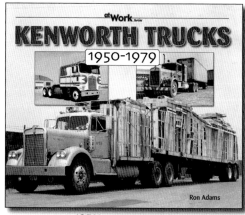
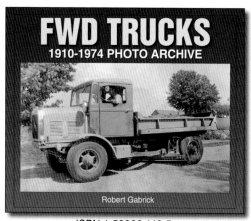

Iconografix, Inc.
P.O. Box 446, Dept BK,
Hudson, WI 54016
For a free catalog call: 1-800-289-3504
info@iconografixinc.com
www.iconografixinc.com